*R*eunion
Your Family

How to Plan It, Organize It, *and* Enjoy It

Your Family Reunion

How to Plan It, Organize It, *and* Enjoy It

George G. Morgan

Library of Congress Cataloging-in-Publication Data

Morgan, George G., 1952-
  Your successful family reunion : organizing a quality family
get-together / by George G. Morgan.
        p. cm.
Includes bibliographical references and index.
  ISBN 0-916489-97-3 (pbk. : acid-free paper)
  1. Family reunions—United States—Planning. I. Title.
GT2424.U5 M67 2001
394.2—dc21

                                        2001002114

Published by Ancestry® Publishing, an
imprint of MyFamily.com, Inc.

P.O. Box 990
Orem, Utah 84059
www.myfamily.com

First Printing 2001
10 9 8 7 6 5 4 3 2 1

Printed in the United States of America

Dedication

*I would like to dedicate this book to families everywhere,
and to the memories of Mary Allen Morgan and Penelope Weatherly,
my two favorite aunts, whose love, gentle elegance, and commitment
to our family shaped each member's life
in so many positive ways.*

Table of Contents

Acknowledgments xi

Introduction: Why Have a Family Reunion? xiii

What Is a Reunion? xiii

Chapter 1

The Size and Scope of Your Reunion 1

   Soliciting Input 1

   What to Do with the Responses .3

   Sizing up the Reunion 4

      A Small Reunion 5

      A Medium-Sized Reunion 5

      Larger Reunions 5

   Location, Location, Location! 6

      The Hometown 6

      Convenient In-Between Location 6

   Timing is Everything! 8

Chapter 2

Organizing for Success 13

   Your Starting Point 14

   Building the Team 16

   The First Meeting 17

   The Next Step: Widening the Circle 20

   Defining a Schedule 21

Chapter 3

Figuring The Cost of a Family Reunion 27

   Reunion Expense Categories .28

      Communications Expense 29

      Location Expenses 30

Mail Tracking Log 159

    Family Reunion Budget Spreadsheet 160

    Registration Follow-up Letter 161

    Family Reunion Evaluation 162

Thank You Letter 163

    Family Genealogy Correction 164

Index 165

About the Author 171

Acknowledgments

Creating a book can be a daunting and exhaustive task involving many hours of planning, research, organizing, writing, rewriting, and other activities. The job is often made easier through the help and support of wonderful people, and this book is no different.

I want to acknowledge and thank the extremely warm, talented and supportive people at MyFamily.com and Ancestry.com for their help and encouragement. Lou Szucs is the greatest executive editor anywhere, and her friendship and belief in this project made it all possible. Juliana Szucs Smith, editor of the *Ancestry Daily News* is my wonderful, loving friend who acted as a sounding board for some of my ideas and helped keep me sane (I owe her bon-bons!). And Jennifer Utley and Matt Wright are undoubtedly the best editors in the business, attentive to all the details and ever ready with excellent advice and words of encouragement.

Thanks also to Drew Smith, my very best friend and the greatest Internet researcher I know, for his steadfast support and help in locating some of the excellent Web resources included in the book.

I want to thank my brother, Carey T. Morgan, for all his love, support, and encouragement through the creative process. Family is important!

And finally I want to thank members of my extended family for some of the best family reunion experiences imaginable. Margaret Morgan Allen, Rita Allen Satterfield, and Beth Morgan Loeb—you are all just terrific!

—George G. Morgan

Why Have a Family Reunion?

Family is important. Contemporary families consist of all types of relationships, from the traditional nuclear family to single parents and domestic partnerships. Our family provides us with a framework of community. Regardless of the makeup of our family, we form all types of relationships within it, ultimately picking out specific family members with whom we develop special relationships. And these group dynamics always seem to have a way of growing and changing over time.

In this fast-paced and complex time in history, family members are often separated by large geographical distances. In addition, our lives are complicated by the unique problems of modern society—all of which create tremendous demands on our time. It is important, however, to maintain connections with our families. Time spent with family members can provide stability and a sense of perspective. In effect, our families can help us reconnect with our intrinsic roots.

There are many motivations for having a family reunion. The most common reason is to bring together family members who have not seen one another for some period of time. Old relationships are renewed and strengthened and new ones can be formed as well. The time frame between these meetings may be short or long, but it is not uncommon for a family reunion to bring people together who may not have seen one another in decades. Two years ago, for instance, I attended a reunion for descendants of my paternal grandfather's brother's family. With only a few exceptions, I had not seen most of these people for over thirty-five years. We had a lot of catching up to do! At that reunion, I formed and reestablished relationships with a number of these relatives, and these relationships have since grown and strengthened.

What Is a Reunion?

Every type of family get-together, from the casual backyard barbecue to a weekend camping trip to a week-long deluxe cruise, can become a "family reunion." The keys to a successful event, however, are to plan and organize a structure for it, get the people together, and provide opportunities for a variety of interactions with one another. Realize from the beginning that you don't have to structure every single minute. You certainly don't even want to try that. Some of the very best interactions are those that are impromptu encounters and get-togethers. They flow naturally and the people involved find something in common that acts as a bond between them—for just that moment or for years to come.

Some people are intimidated by the prospect of organizing a full-scale family reunion. I won't lie to you; it takes a commitment of time and effort to pull it off. It also takes teamwork, family members working together, to make it happen. A successful reunion, however, can be one of the most personally rewarding activities imaginable.

If this is your first time organizing a family reunion, let me suggest that you read the book you now have in your hands from cover to cover before you start. If you've helped organize a family reunion before, you may want to skip around through the chapters, *but* you should read the book from cover to cover to get a full understanding of all the component parts of organizing an even better reunion. And if you've attended a reunion before, and are thinking about volunteering for your next family event, read along and get a feel for how the process works. Once you understand the planning and implementation process, your fear of the unknown will slip quickly behind you and your enthusiasm will surge.

This book is intended as a guide for organizing a successful and memorable family reunion. It includes chapters about getting started with the organization process, determining how to finance the event and work with vendors, deciding where and when to hold it, creating a simple and effective record-keeping system, figuring out how to locate and invite family members, planning opportunities for people of all ages to get to know each other and interact together, setting up the actual reunion site, managing the reunion on-site, and conducting a post-reunion review so that the next one will be even better.

The Internet has changed forever the way we obtain information, and there is a wealth of Web-based reunion sites filled with great information. While you certainly don't need access to the Internet to use this book and organize a successful family reunion, you may want to avail yourself of the many resources to be found online. What if you don't have a computer? Visit your local public library. Most have public access Internet computers, and most librarians will be happy to show you how to use them to search for information on the Web. I have researched vast numbers of Internet sites and have included a number of links to great Web pages I believe will be helpful as you organize your family reunion. You will find these links included in the text and at the end of many chapters. I know you will find these to be helpful supplements to the information in this book. In addition, because Web sites change and because there is so much information on the Internet, you will find Appendix A of especial interest. There I have written a short guide to using Internet search engines, directories, and other tools to locate information. By studying the techniques there and referring to the tutorials at the Search Engine Watch Web site <http://www.searchenginewatch.com>, you can quickly become adept at structuring effective searches for information all over the Internet.

Whatever the motivation for the reunion of your own family, please keep in mind that you're doing it for yourself and for your family. No matter whether this is your first family reunion or your tenth, it is important to do whatever it takes to make your event a smash success—one that your relatives will remember and talk about for the rest of their lives. In fact, this reunion could be the one talked about for generations to come.

Here's wishing you the perfect family reunion!

George G. Morgan
Tampa, FL

Green Berry Holder and his wife, Penelope Swords Holder, hosted the reunion of their twelve children in Rome, Georgia, circa 1905. The author's maternal grandmother, Elizabeth Holder, is shown second from the left in the second row.

The Size and Scope of Your Reunion

Whether you realize it or not, you have probably organized any number of family reunions in the past. In fact, the most typical family reunion occurs quite often over the dinner table. Larger reunions, however, can occur at holiday times, such as Thanksgiving, Christmas, Passover, and in conjunction with birthdays, anniversaries or other important family events. Each of these gatherings involves planning and organizing, attending to details, and communicating with family members in order to invite them to attend. The event itself involves some staging and some on-site management, aspects that are involved in any reunion, regardless of its size.

The size and scope of your family reunion will be determined by a number of factors. These include the number of family members, their ages, where they live, how far they will have to travel, the type of reunion, any special activities you might offer, and the expense involved. You certainly want to plan a reunion that allows the largest number of people to attend.

In This Chapter

- Factors that influence the size of your reunion
- Soliciting necessary input from other family members
- Organizing the input you receive
- Determining reunion size and scope
- Selecting a location for the event
- Using the Internet to assist in your planning

Soliciting Input

The first time you hold a family reunion, it is important to solicit input from family members who are potential attendees. Perhaps the first reunion won't be the full-blown, everyone-in-the-family affair you initially envisioned. It may make sense for the first one to be a local or regional affair for a smaller group of family members. When you hold the event the next time, perhaps word will have spread about how absolutely terrific the first reunion was and more people from a wider geographical area will want to attend. That doesn't mean that they *can't* or *won't* attend the first time; it just means that perhaps the focus should not be on trying to do it all the first time around.

When I say solicit input, I mean you should actively seek out ideas from other family members. Consider this as something of a family brainstorming session. There are multi-

Family Reunion Survey

We are considering holding a family reunion for the descendants of John Paul Jones. In order to determine the interest level among the family and to begin developing a plan, we'd like to get your input concerning this event.

Please answer the questions below, and either mail it to Wally Jones at 123 Maple Lane, Family City, KS 55555 or send it to him via e-mail at wallyjones@address.com.

Your Name: _____

Your Address: _____

_____

Telephone: (____) ____-_____ E-mail: _____@_____

Number of persons in your family: _____

Are you interested in attending a family reunion? YES   NO

What time of year is best for your family to attend? (Please indicate best month)
JAN FEB MAR APR MAY JUNE JULY AUG SEPT OCT NOV DEC

Is there another time you would consider as a second choice? (Please indicate best alternative month)
JAN FEB MAR APR MAY JUNE JULY AUG SEPT OCT NOV DEC

How many persons would be able to attend the reunion?
Adults: _____ Children ages 0-6: _____ Children ages 7-12: _____
Children ages 13-16: _____ Seniors: _____

We are considering having the reunion in Family City, Kansas, because there are so many family members located in that area. Would you attend the reunion if it were held there?   YES   NO

Are there any other areas you would consider as a site for the family reunion?
YES   NO   If so, where? _____

Would you and/or one of your family members be willing to participate on the planning committee for the reunion?   YES   NO   If so, who can participate?
_____

If you cannot help on the planning committee, would you and/or one of your family members be willing to help on-site at the reunion? YES NO
If so, who can participate?

_____

Our reunion will include meals and some commemorative memento of the occasion. There will therefore be a per person cost to attend the reunion that we will communicate to you at a later date. There will be a price for adults and a lower price for children and seniors.

Thank you for your input to the process! We'll communicate the results back to you soon.

Wally Jones

ple ways to solicit input from family members. One is by talking to them, in person or by telephone, to determine the level of interest in the event. Another way is to prepare a simple questionnaire and either mail it, along with a self-addressed, stamped envelope (SASE) to encourage responses, or e-mail it and request electronic responses. A sample questionnaire is included on the opposite page, as well as in Appendix B of this book. The sample provides space to record information about each respondent's interest level, who in each family unit would likely attend, the best time of year to have the reunion, convenient locations, and his or her willingness to participate in working on the reunion. In addition, it asks for contact name, mailing address, telephone number, and e-mail address, all essential for building a family contact database. We'll discuss this database in the next chapter, but suffice it to say that communication is a key element of a successful reunion, and your family contact database is a vital component.

As you begin planning your reunion, it is important to understand the mix of the family members who might attend. Consider planning activities for every age group, from pre-school children to seniors. We'll get to that in a later chapter, but determining the mix of the group at this point is essential to selecting an ideal site for the reunion, developing a budget, setting pricing for attendees, planning meal events, and devising activities to get everyone involved.

What to Do With the Responses

As you receive responses from family members, keep a record of who responded. (We'll talk about record-keeping systems in another chapter, but keep in mind that you want to track who responded and who didn't.) You want to compile and organize these into some semblance of order. If you mailed or e-mailed a questionnaire and receive responses in either of these ways, you may want to group these initially by "I would attend" and "I would not attend." The "woulds" become an active group to prospect, and the "would nots" group becomes an audience to investigate further.

If you solicit input from family members in person or by telephone, be sure to have a copy of the questionnaire in front of you when you do so. It will prompt you to ask the right questions and gather essential information. It also provides a document on which to make notes. Include the name of the person, all of his or her responses, and any additional comments or suggestions he or she may have. Also make a note of the date on which you spoke to the person and whether you spoke in person or by telephone. (Make a note of the telephone number for future reference.) Organize the responses into "woulds" and "would nots" just as you do with the mail or e-mail responses you receive.

The next step is to evaluate the responses you receive. You can do this by hand on a legal pad or you can create a computerized spreadsheet using Microsoft *Excel*™ or some other spreadsheet program. How you tabulate them is irrelevant, but it is important to recognize that the responses you receive are vital to your planning process. Depending on what questions you included in your questionnaire, you want to tabulate and evaluate the responses for each question. For instance, if you ask how many children, adults,

Family Member's name	Would attend	Would not attend	Phone	E-mail	Mail	How many would attend
Alexander, John M.	✓				✓	4
DeJournette, Florence	✓				✓	2
Holder, Edward E	✓		✓			1
Holder, Green Berry		✓			✓	—
Morgan, Samuel T.	✓		✓			6
Morgan, William R.	✓			✓		2

Family Member's Name	Would Attend	Would Not	Phone	E-mail	Mail	How Many
Alexander, John M.	X				X	4
DeJournette, Florence	X				X	2
Holder, Edward E.	X		X			1
Holder, Green Berry		X			X	–
Morgan, Samuel T.	X		X			6
Morgan, William R.	X			X		2

and seniors might attend from a family, you want to tabulate the total number of people in each category so that you can plan any age-related activities. If you include a question about where the reunion should be held, you want to make note of how many people would be willing to travel a specific distance to a specific location to attend the reunion. Got the idea?

Once you've tabulated the results, spend some time studying the information you received. Depending on what you ask, the responses should give you a good indication of the interest level of your family members and how far they are willing to travel to attend the reunion. You may also now have a group of family members who have indicated their willingness to participate in the planning and implementation of the reunion.

Sizing up the Reunion

Now is the time to assess what size of reunion is appropriate for your family group. Again, the first reunion you hold may not be the full-family affair you ultimately hope to produce. The first one may be small, but now is the time to begin determining the size of the reunion. Let's discuss some samples of reunions of various sizes, and what types of activities might be included in each type of event.

A Small Reunion

A small reunion can be a more intimate affair, ranging in size from just a few people to perhaps twenty or twenty-five family members. An event this size can usually be organized and managed quite simply by one to three people. Making any necessary travel and overnight sleeping accommodations for out-of-town relatives may be simplified by having some or all of  them stay in people's homes. There is also the advantage that meals and other events may also be held in someone's home or in a small rented hall. Attendees at a small reunion also have the advantage of getting to know one another better than at a larger reunion. The biggest problem is deciding who to invite.

A smaller reunion might consist of an informal dinner or a barbecue at someone's home. It might be a dinner at a restaurant or a catered meal in a rented hall. And if it is a multi-day event over a weekend in a place where multiple families live, part of the reunion might be held at one family's home and another portion might be held at someone else's home. That way, the burden and responsibility of hosting the event is shared and allows each of the hosts to enjoy some quality leisure time visiting with the family and experiencing the enjoyment of the reunion.

A Medium-Sized Reunion

As the size of a group increases, the planning, organization, and logistical work involved in a family reunion intensifies. A medium-sized reunion probably consists of between twenty-five and fifty attendees. Depending on the age mix of the group, planning can become more complicated as well. Seldom can a group this size be accommodated at someone's home, so it  becomes imperative to locate a venue, such as a hotel, for the event. Sleeping accommodations, transportation to and from the airport, and special events, meals, and other entertainment increase the complexity of the planning *and* the on-site management of the reunion.

Larger Reunions

Large family reunions present some interesting challenges but are also full of rewards. When working with a group of fifty or more people, the amount of advance planning and the lead times required increase. It may be more difficult to locate and schedule hotels and other facilities to accommodate a group of that size unless you work far in advance of the dates. Meals, banquets, entertainment, special events, trans-

portation, and other considerations also will need careful attention. When the size of your group exceeds 100 people, you may even want to consider hiring a professional party planner whose experience and expertise can help guarantee greater success.

Location, Location, Location!

The selection of a good location for your reunion is also a key to its success. The responses you receive from your discussions and questionnaires should provide you with feedback to help you select the most appropriate venue for your reunion. The decision to hold a reunion in a hometown, on a family farm, or in a completely different geographical location can be a difficult one to make. Cost is always a factor, and your choice of a reunion site may, in addition to the actual reunion attendance fee, involve travel and lodging expenses for many family members. Therefore, the location can be one of the most critical decisions of the entire planning process. It will definitely influence whether people will or will not make the trip to attend your family reunion.

The Hometown

Most family members will think of their hometown or some other familiar place from their past as the appropriate venue for holding a family reunion. This can be especially helpful for the reunion planner if he or she and/or other family members still live there. However, if the family has dispersed over the intervening years, this may not be a practical choice. In the event that only a few family members still reside in that area and the vast majority have moved away to other, remote locations, it may be more practical to consider a site that is most convenient to the largest number of people.

Convenient In-Between Location

With family members spread from one end of the country to another, or to other countries around the globe, it may be impractical or unfair to expect them to travel an inordinately long distance to attend a family reunion. The time and expense involved can be prohibitive, and lengthy travel with children or elderly family members may be a daunting task. Therefore, it may make sense to select a convenient in-between location. This may add to the overall expense of the reunion because one or more of the planners will need to visit the place where the reunion is to be held, meet with hotel and catering sales staffs, and make other arrangements in advance of the reunion. The planners and any additional family volunteers will also need to arrive a day or two in advance of the reunion to finalize all the arrangements, coordinate set-up, and take control of the implementation and management of the affair.

On the other hand, selection of a neutral facility at a convenient in-between location may provide just the right site for an even more enjoyable reunion. Of course, you should always consider the age mix of the group to ensure that there is something for everyone who attends. Here are some examples of places you might choose:

Big Cities - You might decide that a big city such as New York, Chicago, Washington, D.C., Denver, Houston, Los Angeles, San Francisco, or some other large urban destination is just the place for a fun-filled reunion. Cities offer a broad choice in accommodations for your reunion, as well as lots of entertainment opportunities. The downside is that the excitement of visiting a large city may distract people and cause them to cut out to sightsee rather than focus on the reunion.

Resorts - There are many types of resorts offering a wide variety of options for the reunion planner. Depending on your family and its interests, you might consider a family resort such as Disney World in Orlando, Florida, with its scores of hotels and multiple theme parks. Some resorts offer golfing, tennis, and other sports. Still others provide spas, exercise, and/or relaxation facilities. When it comes to this venue option, there really is something for everyone.

Parks and Recreational Facilities - Many families use parks, nature preserves, hiking and climbing facilities, and other outdoor places for their reunions. Starting with local parks and nature preserves, some families organize reunion picnics and sporting events as single-day activities. These usually require obtaining a permit from the local government or park service and arriving early to reserve a choice spot for the group. Other families organize trips to national parks for the purpose of camping, boating, whitewater rafting, swimming, hiking, biking, and any number of other activities. They may travel by car, trailer, or camper. Families carry their own provisions and prepare their own meals, and they may choose to sleep out under the stars. Certainly this venue is not for everyone, but it may be an ideal family reunion opportunity for a family of able-bodied individuals who enjoy these kinds of outdoor activities.

Vacations and Holiday Trips - Your family may decide to take a trip and meet up with other family members at another location for a holiday. Our family, for instance, used to meet at Myrtle Beach, South Carolina every Thanksgiving and would be joined by my mother's two remaining sisters and their families. We rented several condominium apartments in a high-rise building on the oceanfront, cooked breakfast in and ate all other meals out, and spent five wonderful days together on a beautiful beach.

Ski Trip – Winter and snow enthusiasts may want to consider a family ski trip reunion. While not everyone is a skier, there are lots of activities scheduled in ski lodge resorts. You might even decide to rent a house and live as a communal family. The skiers can hit the slopes while the non-skiers shop, take tours, or just relax and visit in front of a roaring fire.

Ranches - A family retreat to a dude ranch may be just the ticket for a fun-filled, active outdoor experience. Riding, hiking, and other activities provide the flavor of ranch life for the group.

Cruises - An oceangoing cruise or an excursion down the Mississippi River can provide a scenic experience for family members of all ages. Group rates are often available that include discounted airfares and other good deals. Cruise ships typically provide delicious food, which relieves you of the responsibility of meal planning, and there are on-board activities for all ages.

Special Family Events - Some families organize their reunions around special events. These might include family milestone events such as a wedding, a christening or baptism, a *bar mitzvah/bat mitzvah*, a golden wedding anniversary, a graduation, the placement of a family monument or memorial, commemoration of an historical event in which an ancestor was involved, the dedication or rededication of a family church, or some other event. Let your imagination transport you from there!

Timing Is Everything!

Now that you know how to go about soliciting information about your relatives' interest in a reunion, gaining some feeling about sizes of reunions, and developing some ideas about locations, let's talk about how to select the date for your family reunion.

If location is a critical concern in planning a family reunion, timing is equally as important. Most reunion planners choose the summertime for their events for several reasons. First, the weather is more dependable and lends itself to many outdoor activities. More importantly, most children are out of school and parents have increased flexibility in scheduling their vacation time. Holiday times, however, can also work well for reunions. If you're planning a reunion with lots of outdoor activities, summer may be your best option. If you are considering a reunion at a ski lodge, though, you certainly won't find good snow conditions in North America in the summertime.

One of the critical questions you must ask in your questionnaire concerns timing for the reunion. You want to plan the event so that the most family members can attend. Therefore, place a high degree of emphasis on the information you receive regarding timing to help assure a higher attendance rate.

As you evaluate the timeframe for your reunion, consider the location *and* the time of year in your planning. Visiting the Alamo in Texas in August coincides with the height of summer heat and humidity, and people may not attend the reunion because they anticipate uncomfortable weather conditions. On the other hand, October in New England may be a big draw because the weather is tolerable and the autumn colors are spectacular. And Denver in January is probably a poor choice of venue unless you are planning events focusing on snow-related activities.

As you can see, reunions can come in many sizes and locations, and can happen for many reasons. Your family reunion will be as unique as your family and its members. Again, the input received from your family members as a result of conversations, questionnaires, and other means of communication is essential. It will help you determine the level of interest your family members have in a reunion and its location, and will give you a good idea of the age mix of potential attendees. All of these component pieces of information will help you formulate a good idea for what type of reunion is appropriate for *your* family.

As I mentioned earlier, you must always maintain an awareness of who your audience is. The mix of people in your family, their interests, their ages, and their abilities or disabilities should play a large part in influencing your decisions concerning the location, time of year, and events you choose for your family reunion.

The importance of the solicitation of input from family members who might attend the reunion should now be pretty obvious to you. Now that you have that data and some resources to begin exploring location, it's time to consider how to organize the reunion. Chances are you won't be able to do it by yourself; it requires help and teamwork from other family members. With that in mind, let's proceed to the next chapter.

Questions to Ask Yourself

- What are the factors that influence the size of our family's reunion?

- What method(s) of soliciting input from our family members will we be using?

- What questions will we ask on our questionnaire?

- Who will review the responses, and how will we organize them?

- How large will our reunion be and who will we invite?

- Where will we hold the reunion?

- Who has access to the Internet and will we use it to locate resources to help in our planning process?

Internet Resources
Locations and Facilities for Your Family Reunion

Venues

The Internet can provide a lot of assistance in selecting potential locations for your family reunion. Begin your exploration of possible venues by visiting Web sites related to the travel and entertainment industry. Here are some good places to start:

Reunion Research - Reunion Sites -

- http://www.reuniontips.com/sites.html - This site contains a compiled list, by ZIP code, of hotels, condominiums, ranches, campgrounds, convention centers, and other commercial entities actively seeking your reunion business.

FamilyReunion.com - Resources -

- http://www.familyreunion.com/resources/ - This site uses a search engine and contains links to help you locate helpful resources for your family reunion. The hospitality, travel, catering, and rentals categories are particularly helpful.

Reunion Magazine's Online Resources -

- http://www.reunionsmag.com/_old/reunion_resources.html - *Reunion Magazine* is a good publication for family reunion planners. Its Web site contains a great collection of hotels and other hospitality facilities, group by state. Explore the rest of its Web site for ideas and links to destination and facility resources.

Travel and Entertainment

The following categories of links can help you locate travel agents, hotels, resorts, and other venues for your family reunion.

Travel and Tourism

- American Society of Travel Agents - http://www.astanet.com
- Association of Canadian Travel Agents - http://www.acta.net
- Travelocity.com - http://www.travelocity.com
- Yahoo! Travel - http://travel.yahoo.com

Resorts

- Hotels, Resorts, and Inns - http://hotels.about.com/travel/hotels
- Resorts and Lodges - http://www.resortsandlodges.com
- Resorts OnLine - http://www.resortsonline.com

Parks and Recreational Facilities

- Great Outdoor Recreation Pages (GORP) - U.S. National Parks Guides
http://www.gorp.com/gorp/resource/US_National_Park/main.htm
- National Park Service - National Park Guide - http://www.nps.gov/parks.html
- Yahoo! Parks - http://parks.yahoo.com

Ranches

- Family Farms and Dude Ranches -
http://travelwithkids.about.com/travel/travelwithkids/cs/farmsduderanches
- Great Outdoor Recreation Pages (GORP) - Dude Ranches -
http://gorptravel.gorp.com/dude_search_main.asp

Ski Trips

- SKI Magazine - http://www.skimag.com
- SkiMaps.com - http://www.skimaps.com
- Yahoo! Ski & Snow - http://snow.yahoo.com

Cruises

- Excite Travel: Cruises & Vacations -
http://www.excite.com/travel/cruises_and_vacations
- Expedia Cruises Home Page - http://cruises.expedia.com

Miscellaneous Map and Travel Sites

- MapQuest - http://www.mapquest.com
- Travelocity.com - http://www.travelocity.com
- Yahoo! Maps and Driving Directions - http://maps.yahoo.com
- Yahoo! Travel - http://travel.yahoo.com

Smith Family Reunion, 1996

Chapter 2

Organizing for Success

In Chapter 1, we discussed soliciting input from family members regarding their interest in a family reunion, the best time of year to hold it, and a convenient location for the event. We also focused on the importance of understanding the age mix of the family members, from preschoolers to seniors, and planning activities that include everyone in the family. Now that you have that information, it is time to begin organizing in order to create a successful and memorable family reunion.

The keys to a successful family reunion are planning and organization. The first thing to understand is that you cannot do it alone. You may be a master organizer and possess the skills necessary to perform all the tasks associated with the family reunion, but you will still need help from other people. In order to stage a successful family reunion, you also must recognize that other family members need and want to be involved. Involving family members in the planning and organization processes for the family reunion accomplishes that on a number of levels.

First of all, by enlisting family members in the planning process, you gain their perspectives and ideas. It is impossible for you to know everything about every family member who might attend the reunion. People have different interests and therefore have different ideas about what will and will not constitute a good time. Involving people of different families, different geographic areas, different ages, and different interests, you are sure to get ideas and suggestions that add dynamic possibilities to your planning.

Second, everyone has a different set of skills. One person may be great with finances and would make a great treasurer. Someone may be a computer expert who can build a family name and address database, create attractive mailers and invitations, and produce mailing labels, nametags, signs, and other computerized materials. Another person may

In this Chapter

- Why organization is the key to any successful reunion
- Getting help
- Building a core planning team
- Assigning responsibilities and setting schedules
- The importance of status reports
- Internet resources that can help

have had experience working with hoteliers and caterers and therefore may be able to help plan and coordinate banquets and other food events. Yet another person may be wonderful with children and can help plan entertaining activities and events for them. You will want to draw on the many skills and talents within your family for these and other types of activities.

Finally, involving family members can pique their interest and ensure their buy-in for the reunion. If they have a stake in the planning and organization process, they are almost certain to attend. In addition, they become additional word-of-mouth communicators, telling other family members how great the reunion is going to be and encouraging them to attend.

As you can see, the planning and organization process can involve many facets. You certainly want the reunion to be a success, but you don't want to be personally overwhelmed. You will also want to enjoy the reunion yourself. By enlisting the help and support of other family members in the planning and organization process, you can build an unbeatable team that will make the reunion an unqualified success. At the same time, you have the opportunity to help create, build, and expand relationships between family members as they work together on the event.

This chapter is devoted to describing how to go about organizing for success. It presents a step-by-step approach to building a family team to help you plan and orchestrate a terrific family reunion. With that in mind, let's look at this simple methodology.

Your Starting Point

The best starting point for organizing your family reunion is to begin with a rough idea of what you think the family reunion should be. If you followed the suggestions presented in the last chapter, you obtained input for the reunion from other family members. You solicited that information by using a questionnaire sent via mail or e-mail or communicated through telephone interviews. With the information you obtained, you should now be able to sketch out what you and the other family members think would make a great family reunion.

You have to ask yourself some questions. Should it be a one-day, weekend, or week-long event? Should it be in your hometown or in another location, at someone's home or at a hotel or resort, or do you have another idea altogether? Will it involve inviting every member from every branch of the family or a smaller group? If it is to be a smaller group, who will be included and how will you make that determination? Will it be an adults-only event or will children be included? What types of events will comprise the reunion?

The answers to these questions like these will help you develop the "stake in the ground" to begin your discussions and planning for your successful family reunion. Remember, whatever you do, don't limit yourself to the first ideas you jot down on paper. These are only your starting point, and they should provide a focus for your initial discussions.

The next step is to summarize the information and your notes into a single document. Organize your notes and compile them into an outline. Include notes from the questionnaire responses you received for clarification. For instance, one bullet in your outline might concern the potential location where the reunion might be held. You might include a note in your outline indicating that eight people responded to the question that they preferred the family reunion to be held at grandma's house in the old hometown, while three people suggested Aunt Elizabeth's home in another city, and two suggested holding the reunion at Disney World. This outline document (see example below) becomes the first working document for your team's use in deciding the type of reunion, the location, and the activities to be held. With an initial focus defined, you are now ready to begin enlisting family members to participate on your reunion team.

Reunion Planning Summary

The following is a summary of the responses from our survey regarding our family reunion.

Preference for a place for the reunion:

Grandma Smith's house	8 responses
Aunt Elizabeth Weatherly's house	3 responses
Disney World in Orlando, FL	6 responses
Kansas City, MO (mid-point)	9 responses
No preference	1 response

Preference for time of year for the reunion:

June	11 responses
July	3 responses
August	9 responses
September	2 responses
No preference	2 responses

Estimated number of adults attending: 34

Estimated number of seniors attending: 13

Estimated number of children attending:

Ages 0-6	3
Ages 7-12	9
Ages 13-16	7
Total =	19

People expressing a willingness in participating on the planning committee:
John Swords - Mailing list and invitations
Ed Smith - Accounting and finance
Laura Wilson - Catering and food., menus, etc.
John Alexander, Jr. - Willing to work with hotel
Cathy Wilson and Beth Smith - Decorations
Marie McKnitt - Family history and genealogy
Walt Weatherly, Sam Morgan, Emma Dale Holder, Edith Morgan, Peter Frank, Murray West, and Lydia Wilson - Willing to be assigned as needed

The following are some other ideas for the reunion:

Ideas regarding commemorative items:
T-shirt
Coffee mug
Sports water bottle
Group photograph

Suggested activities
Icebreaker games
Photo and heirloom display
Family history display
Pizza party for the younger set
Trip to see the old family home and the family cemetery
Softball, horseshoes, and badminton games
Banquet

Building the Team

The size of your team will depend on a number of factors. These include the size of your reunion, the location, its duration, the types and scope of the events you plan, and the skills and talents of your family members.

You should have received a lot of information from other family members you solicited during the questionnaire process. One of the questions you asked was whether the respondent would be interested in participating in planning and organizing the

---

Would you and/or one of your family members be willing to participate on the planning committee for the reunion? (YES) NO If so, who can participate?

_____ Edward E. Holder _____

If you cannot help on the planning committee, would you and/or one of your family members be willing to help on-site at the reunion? YES NO
If so, who can participate?

---

reunion. The people who responded in the affirmative provide an excellent starting point for your planning team. You will want your initial planning committee to be a relatively small group, typically three to five individuals to help you shape the initial plans for the reunion. These people should have a good general knowledge of the family and its members. Once the general direction of the family reunion is set, they can continue their participation and/or recommend others with particular skill sets to join the planning and organization team.

Start by making telephone contact with the people who indicated their willingness to participate and confirm that they are still interested in helping plan and organize the reunion. If they are, tell them you have an initial document with ideas about the reunion that you would like to send to them for review. Suggest two or three possible dates and times for the first meeting of this family reunion planning committee. If any of the committee members are located out of town, you may want to invest in a speakerphone. If you have multiple people in other locations, you may want to contact your telephone company and subscribe to the three-way calling service for the duration of the time until your reunion. You can invite people who live near you to your home for the meetings and use your speakerphone and three-way calling to conduct effective meetings. You will find that this method of communication will save you a substantial amount of time in communicating and re-communicating information among your team. Everyone has the opportunity to hear information presented first-hand and can participate freely in the discussions.

As you make contact with each potential team member, you will want to record his or her name, address, e-mail address, and telephone number. While you may think you have the correct, current information for everyone, remember that telephone numbers, area codes, and e-mail addresses frequently change. (You will find a Family Contact Form in Appendix B of this book for use in gathering correct family information.)

The next step is to make contact with each person again to set the date and time of the first meeting. It is your responsibility now to get a copy of your document into each person's hands and provide them with ample opportunity to review it prior to the meeting. Let each person know how you plan to get the document to them, e.g., deliver it, snail-mail it, e-mail it, or fax it. Make sure you provide enough lead time for the document to arrive and for the team member to review it. In addition, prepare an agenda for the meeting and include it with the planning document. We will discuss more details on that later.

The First Meeting

The first meeting of your planning team can set the tone for the reunion. You want it to be a pleasant experience with ample opportunity for the communication and sharing of information and ideas. The document you prepared should have provided a good summary of the information-gathering process you conducted. The participants at your first meeting should therefore have an understanding of the ideas and desires expressed by other family members during the questionnaire process.

Start your meeting by thanking everyone for agreeing to participate in this first planning session. Since you conducted the information-gathering process, it might be appropriate to briefly review your document and ask if there are any questions. Offer to share any details from the questionnaires with the members of your team. Remember, it is essential for them to understand as much as you do about the requests, ideas, and suggestions made by the people who responded to the questionnaire. You might ask for a volunteer to act as a secretary and take notes during the meeting for future reference.

Begin the planning process by setting some goals for your first meeting. You should have prepared an agenda for the meeting that lists topics and/or goals. The agenda will set expectations for the team regarding the action items that need to be addressed during the meeting. It is also a tool to help you bring focus to the team, especially if people get off topic. Your agenda might include the following topics:

- Discuss the viability of having a family reunion
- Determine the duration of the reunion
- Determine a location for the reunion
- Determine potential dates for the reunion (first, second and third choices)
- Determine who will be invited to the reunion (scope and size)
- Define primary areas of responsibility for the reunion

- Assign responsibilities to team members present
- Identify other family members who might be recruited to help, the skills they bring to the table, and what responsibilities they might assume
- Set the date and time for the next meeting

With the primary goals of this first meeting defined, ask for comments and suggestions from your team members. It might be a good idea to have a flip chart and markers available for notes, and encourage people participating by telephone to set aside a piece of paper for notes. As you make notes on the flip chart, you will want to clearly state to the telephone participants what you are writing. You want to keep everyone in sync.

You will find during the first meeting that people will be full of ideas and suggestions. Your role will be to act as facilitator and moderator of the meeting. Don't necessarily rule out or ignore suggestions. What might initially seem like a wild or impossible idea may actually turn out to be, in some incarnation, a brilliant stroke of genius. Encourage people to brainstorm, but also try to keep them on topic. Keep referring to your agenda or goals to bring people back to focus on specific items  for discussion. You may not get through your entire agenda in this first meeting, in which case you may need to schedule another conference. This will be easier now that you have all or most of your core team gathered together. You may also want to begin assigning action items to be accomplished prior to the next meeting.

Depending on the size and scope of the reunion you plan to host, there will be a number of areas of responsibility. You will want to discuss these during your first meeting or schedule a separate meeting specifically to discuss them. Following is a list of responsibilities and major task assignments for your reunion. We will cover these in more detail later in the book, but the list provides points for discussion during your initial meeting.

Family Contact Database - Compile information on each family unit and its members including names, address, telephone, e-mail, and other data for use in communicating about the reunion and possibly for the creation of a family directory.

Communication - Create and mail letters, postcards, flyers, and other materials (printed and electronic) to communicate and promote information about the reunion.

Registration Tracking - Receive, record, track, and report individual and family registrations for the reunion.

Finances - Develop the budget for the reunion, receive monies from family members for registrations, issue receipts as necessary, pay bills, track expenditures, prepare financial reports, and communicate/work with other team members regarding finances associated with their respective activities and responsibilities.

Hotel Facilities and Accommodations - Work with hotels to negotiate pricing for sleeping accommodations and/or meeting room space required.

Food and Catering - Work with family members, hoteliers, and caterers to develop menus for events involving food, negotiate pricing, and to plan and coordinate set-up.

Transportation - Arrange for the on-site transportation needs of attendees at the reunion. This might involve pick-up at the airport or arranging for a tour bus for family excursions.

Entertainment - Arrange for entertainment during the reunion. This might include engaging a band or a DJ, coordinating a cocktail/mixer party, developing entertainment for children and teenagers, and/or developing and coordinating family excursions to nearby points of interest or entertainment.

On-site Reunion Management - Coordinate and manage the reunion logistics on-site. This might include setting up and staffing the registration desk, coordinating decorations for events, distributing nametags and newsletters, setting up and changing signage, handling any security and crowd management activities, and a host of other essential activities that ensure the reunion goes smoothly.

Recording the Events - Make arrangements for photography/videography to record events at the reunion. Negotiate rates for these services and make arrangements for family members to obtain copies of photographs and videos after the reunion at reasonable rates.

Information Gathering of Family Information - Gather up-to-date contact information on all attendees for the reunion files and for a family address book. Gather genealogical data for family historical purposes and facilitate the recording and sharing of such information.

This list may be too detailed for a simple family reunion, or it may be perfect for a mid-sized reunion. Depending on your own family reunion, and on the interests of your attendees, there may indeed be other activities that require the assignment of responsibility. For instance, some families like to engage in a family talent show, and this would require an additional committee responsible for scouting out talent, obtaining and setting up a venue for the show, arranging for music and decorations, etc. The list above, however, should give you an idea of the types of activities requiring attention and which activities an individual or committee group may need to be assigned responsibilities.

The team members present at your initial meeting may have a great deal to discuss and suggest about the areas of responsibilities the group identifies. A next step would be to ask the question, "For which of these areas could you or would you take responsibility?" It is now that there is usually the pregnant pause in conversation. Up to this point, everyone has been full of ideas and suggestions. Your role as moderator now includes enlisting the core members of your team to take responsibility for one or more areas. You can facilitate this by asking a second question, "Who do we know in the family who could or would do a great job with some of these responsibilities?" This usually spurs a discussion of family members who would be great at specific tasks and others whom you would not want to ask. Ultimately, however, you want to ask the team members present, "Can you help by contacting so-and-so, explain what we need in order to put on the family reunion, and ask if he or she would be willing to help in a particular area?" Now the attendees of your initial planning meeting have become core team members, buying into the reunion and taking responsibility for additional team-building activities.

The Next Step: Widening the Circle

In order to reach this juncture, you may have held one initial planning meeting or it may have required two meetings. However, by now you have probably accomplished everything on your agenda that you can by yourselves. Your reunion has probably begun to take on a specific shape and the excitement level is probably very high. With specific ideas in mind and areas of responsibility defined, the next step is for you and your core team members to begin contacting other family members to participate in the planning and development process. A word of warning, though: you don't want too many people involved in the planning process. The old adage about too many cooks and what it can do to the broth certainly holds true. What you want are committee chairpersons to accept responsibility for specific areas. They need to be brought up to speed with plans for the reunion, after which they can develop specific plans for their own areas of responsibility and report back. Set a date at your first meeting for a follow-up meeting to bring new members on-board and to continue the planning process with their involvement.

One person, perhaps two, needs to act as the "president, " or chairperson of the reunion committee. That person (or persons) should be the visionary who maintains an overall view of the reunion and where it's going. You should consider a hierarchical organization for your reunion committee structure. There should be regular meetings and regular reports on the status of projects and activities. Another essential individual for your team is the secretary, who should take notes and summarize meetings and provide copies of minutes as necessary. Depending on the reunion you are planning, these notes may be as informal or detailed as you and your planning team deem appropriate.

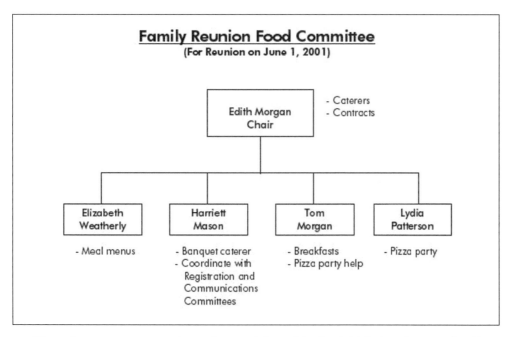

Allow the core team members who participated in the initial planning meeting(s) to make contact with and recruit family members for specific areas of responsibility. Give them time to explain the plans and the direction of the reunion, but set a schedule for locating family members to help with the reunion. Encourage cross-communication and additional brainstorming between one another. In the formative stages of the reunion, it may be difficult to recruit other family members to participate and help. It is not unusual for some frustration to seep in and it is important for team members to provide support to one another to maintain the high level of excitement and enthusiasm necessary to really get the ball rolling. Your reunion *will* be successful; it is simply a matter of building and maintaining enthusiasm and momentum.

Defining a Schedule

Once additional family members have been enlisted to participate in helping with the reunion, they need to be given a schedule or time line. You cannot expect the reunion to organize itself, and you cannot expect everyone to figure out on their own when their tasks must be completed. In order to develop an effective, workable time line, you need input from the people taking responsibility for their given area(s). These are the people with the experience and/or skill sets to successfully do the job and you must depend on their expertise. Therefore, ask each person to prepare a chronological list of activities associated with their area of responsibility. Place the emphasis on "chronological." Each person will certainly be working on their area of responsibility while others are working on theirs. It will be the chairperson's job to monitor the progress of the event; he or she will need to act as coordinator for the entire project. Invariably, there are activities that are dependent on one other, and the successful completion of one activity may be required before a second one can begin or before a third can be completed. It is there-

Family Reunion
Food Committee Schedule
(For Reunion on June 1, 2001)

DATES	DESCRIPTION	RESPONSIBLE
01/05/01	Determine number and types of meal functions	Committee
01/21/01	Develop ideas for sample menus for all meals for all age groups	Eliz. & Lydia
02/01/01	Contact caterers for banquet proposals	Edith & Harriett
02/18/01	Identify and contact family members regarding hosting breakfasts at their homes	Tom & Elizabeth
03/01/01	Receive all caterers' proposals in writing for banquet	Edith & Harriett
03/16/01	Evaluate all caterers' proposals and select caterer for banquet	Edith & Harriett
03/16/01	Work with family members to finalize breakfast menus	Elizabeth & Tom
03/16/01	Request contract from caterer for banquet	Edith & Harriett
04/01/01	Finalize menu with caterer and sign contract	Edith & Harriett
04/30/01	Obtain final counts of reunion attendees in all age groups from Registration Committee	Harriett
05/01/01	Contact Paula's Pizza Palace re: pizzas for youngsters' pizza party	Lydia
05/01/01	Communicate final banquet counts & number of tables to Decorations & Signage Committee	Edith & Eliz.
05/01/01	Communicate all details to the Comm. Committee for inclusion in Attendee Packet	Harriett
05/14/01	Communicate final counts to caterer	Harriett
05/18/01	Communicate final counts to host families for breakfasts	Tom
06/02/01	Order pizzas, host pizza party at reunion, and clean up afterwards	Lydia & Tom
06/02/01	Meet with caterer on-site before banquet	Edith & Harriett
06/02/01	Host our reunion banquet - 7:00 PM	Committee

fore important that project status be communicated in some fashion on a regular basis. This can take the form of a status meeting, a written report, an e-mail, or a telephone call. The chairperson determines what format is appropriate.

When all the participants have completed their chronological list of activities for their area(s) of responsibility, the list should be submitted to the overall chairperson and/or the core team. Each list should be reviewed and the activities should be incorporated into a calendar, with due dates assigned for each activity. Dependencies (activities dependent on the completion of other activities) should be noted, and milestones and their due dates should be assigned. Milestones are typically those drop-dead activities that are "stoppers" for other activities. Once all the activities have been identified, dependencies have been noted, and milestones' due dates have been assigned, it is appropriate to develop an all-inclusive reunion schedule. Be sure to list status report due dates in the schedule. The schedule will act as a timeline for the entire reunion. It should be distributed to all your team members so that they can then see the tasks for which they are responsible and how they relate to the overall reunion schedule. Encourage your team members to highlight their items.

Your team members may choose to recruit other family members as their helpers. Encourage your team members to share the schedule with everyone involved so that there is a clear understanding of what needs to be done in order to accomplish all the activities to make your reunion a success.

Regular status reports are a very important part of your reunion schedule. As you build the schedule, be certain to include status report dates. From the very beginning, stick to the dates and establish a follow-up schedule. If a report is not received on its due date, be prepared to make contact the next day to ask for the report. It is important to set this precedent from the beginning because missed deadlines or volunteers who drop out can compound and spell disaster. The earlier you know you have a problem, the better prepared you will be to address and correct it.

This may sound like a lot of work, and it is. However, it is not overwhelming, especially when you have help. Planning and organizing a family reunion the first time is a learning experience. It is good to have other family members with whom to share it. As you can see, there can be a lot of pieces to a family reunion and you want some help to make it happen. Developing the details in each area takes a lot of time and effort. A core team of enthusiastic and supportive family members working in concert with one another can plan and organize a very successful reunion. You have to build a schedule, stick to it, anticipate problems, monitor status, and maintain enthusiasm and support for your team throughout the project. It's going to be a great family reunion!

Now that we've discussed planning and organization, and a project management structure that can work for you, the following chapters will address the areas of responsibility we discussed in this chapter and provide suggestions for how to be successful in each one.

Questions to Ask Yourself

- Which family members can and will help organize the reunion?

- What family members are good with finances, computer software, working with caterers and other vendors, gathering and maintaining information?

- Who is our family genealogist?

- Can we develop a realistic schedule?

- How often will we check our progress via status reports and what form will the reporting take?

- Have I considered Internet resources to help our planning efforts?

Internet Resources

To Help You Organize Your Reunion

Better Homes and Gardens

- Planning a Successful Family Reunion
  http://www.bhglive.com/food/cookhelpers/reunion/ reunion8.html

Family-Reunion.com

- http://www.family–reunion.com

FamilyReunion.com

- http://www.familyreunion.com

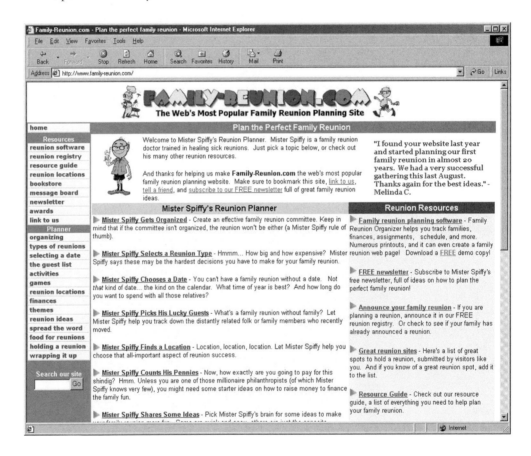

Burgon Family Reunion, 1920

Chapter 3

Figuring the Cost of a Family Reunion

Money matters! You cannot stage an effective family reunion without money. At the same time, you probably cannot afford to spend an unlimited amount of your own or other family members' money on the reunion. Throughout the entire planning process, money matters will remain a constant consideration.

A successful family reunion depends on sound financial planning from the start. You certainly don't want to skimp on the essentials and host a tacky reunion, but you also don't want to go overboard and waste money on unnecessary gimmicks either. From the outset, it is important to develop and maintain a sound, solid budget for the reunion. This means preparing a list of all potential areas where there may be costs involved, preparing a list of each component, obtaining estimates for and researching the cost of each component, and preparing a realistic budget for each area. For example, you might want to investigate the area of additional entertainment for the reunion. If you were considering an excursion to an amusement park, you will want to investigate the cost of the charter van or bus transportation and the expected gratuity for the driver(s), the price of admission to the park, the cost of box lunches for everyone, and any other expenses. In addition, you would want to obtain estimates from several transportation companies and references from previous customers. After preparing a budget for the overall reunion, determine whether a contingency factor is necessary and add that into the budget. Once you've arrived at your final budgetary figure, you can then determine a per-person cost to use as your reunion registration fee.

In the last chapter, we discussed the importance of building a team and recruiting the assistance of other family members. We also discussed assigning responsibilities based on experience, expertise, and talent. As you develop your budget, team members experienced working with hotels and/or caterers, organizing trips and events involving transportation, hiring and supervising DJs and photographers, etc. can be assigned responsibilities for gathering information to help in the budget planning process.

Your definition of the size and scope of the reunion is your starting point for planning a solid budget. For instance, if you decide that your family reunion will take the form of a picnic in a park with twenty-five people in attendance, your budget will certainly be much different than a budget for a reunion held at a hotel or resort with 100 people in attendance where the costs of meeting rooms, banquets, and other expenses must be calculated.

You and your team members can do a great deal of advance research and comparison shopping by telephone and on the Internet. It is imperative, however, that you choose one person to act as treasurer who is responsible to regularly review and update the financial records and identify any potential problems before they get out of control. Your treasurer should probably have another person acting as a co-treasurer/assistant to share the duties. Multiple people should have signature authority for any bank accounts.

In this chapter, we will talk in detail about different categories of reunion expenses and how to evaluate them. We will then discuss how to develop a realistic budget and how to build an effective financial record-keeping system to keep track of ongoing expenses. In addition, you will find a sample budget in Appendix B of this book that can serve as a starting point for planning the budget for your own reunion. You can customize it to fit your reunion by adding and/or removing budgetary items.

Reunion Expense Categories

Every family reunion is unique. The type of reunion you decide to host—its size, location, and the amenities you choose to offer—will directly influence the overall cost of the event. There are, however, various categories of expenses that remain common to all reunions and we will discuss each of these in detail. These categories include:

- Communications
- Location
- Permits and licenses
- Catering/food
- Transportation

- Hired personnel
- Decorations and signage
- Commemorative clothing
- Supplies and equipment

Each category is a distinct entity and should be treated accordingly. For budget planning purposes, you may choose to assign responsibility for each category to a committee of one or more individuals. It will become their responsibility to gather detailed information and compile a profile of component items and their costs, and to make recommendations to the overall reunion planning committee.

Communications Expense

Communication with the planning and organization team and with other family members is a key component of a successful reunion. There are costs associated with most forms of these communications. Let's look at the types of communications that are necessary for a successful family reunion.

Telephone – The telephone is a key communication tool in planning a family reunion. Planners and organizers will use the telephone frequently to talk with one another, and they will use it to contact other family members for such things as the survey mentioned previously in this book, clarification of registration details, coordination of schedules and events, and a myriad of other details. It is unreasonable to expect reunion planners to absorb the cost of additional telephone usage, especially long distance telephone charges.

Instead, budget funds for telephone expenses up front and ask people to supply photocopies of their telephone bills with long distance and toll calls highlighted. You also might consider creating a simple expense account sheet specifically for telephone charges. People can then submit the expense account sheet and a copy of their long distance telephone bill as a means of requesting reimbursement. This becomes documentation for your financial files.

Mailing Materials, Copies, and Postage – One of the major expenses of a family reunion is mailings. Beginning with the initial survey and continuing with each subsequent mailing, the reunion committee will incur expenses associated with producing the survey, making photocopies, placing the survey in envelopes and enclosing self addressed, stamped envelopes (SASEs), producing and applying mailing and return address labels, and applying postage to the entire package. A typical reunion committee will make four to five general mailings:

1. The survey to determine interest level
2. Initial announcement of the reunion
3. Invitation and registration packet (includes family contact form to elicit up-to-date information)
4. Follow-up mailing to remind people to return their registrations
5. Final reminder before the reunion (build the hype)

As you prepare your budget, you must take into consideration the price of postage for each mailing. Be aware of any postal rate increases announced by the government.

You can encourage responses for your initial survey and for registration by enclosing SASEs, and this adds to your expense. You may slightly reduce your postage expense by using an oversized postcard for your final reminder mailing.

E-mail - Electronic mail is an inexpensive and effective way to communicate with people. You may consider this communication method for day-in and day-out communication with other team members. You may even consider it for some or all of your communication with some of your more computer-savvy family members. However, printed mailings that incorporate graphics and fonts will make a substantial visual impact with the recipients and pique their interest. You will also find that snail-mail (standard mail) is most effective with registration packets. This is because it provides materials with visual impact that can be looked at and passed around to other members of the family, materials that might be otherwise lost or deleted if sent via e-mail. The printed and mailed package usually generates a sense of excitement and anticipation that may be lost with text-only e-mail. A majority of your family members, unless they are older, will already have access to e-mail. Those who do not have e-mail today but who have access to the Internet can always obtain a free e-mail account at places on the Web such as Yahoo!, Juno, and a variety of other Internet sites.

Location Expenses

Unless you are hosting your family reunion at someone's home, in a park, or in a free hall, the cost of the location in which to host your family reunion can be the largest single expense in your budget. Let's discuss several scenarios.

Someone's Home - Many reunions are held in someone's home. My cousin Rita has volunteered the use of her home for a number of her family's reunions. She has a lovely home on a terrific farm near Roxboro, North Carolina, next door to her mother's home. The farm has a beautiful, expansive front and side yard with huge trees creating a park-like atmosphere. The reunion is usually held on a Sunday afternoon in mid-September when the weather is dependable. Everyone brings a covered dish or some homemade family recipe, along with lawn chairs for their group. Typically, there are seventy-five to 100 people in attendance, and family members help set up beforehand and clean up afterward. As a result, the location cost for this reunion is negligible.

Picnic in the Park - Your family may decide to hold its reunion as a picnic in a park of some type. Parks with picnic grounds sometimes have pavilions and these can be ideal places for family get-togethers. Facilities of this type usually require some advance reservations so it is wise to contact the county or municipal body responsible for the park to determine the requirements. Sometimes there is a flat fee for the use of the facility or, in other cases, a refundable deposit may be required.

Church Hall - One option for a reunion is the use of a hall at a religious institution. If you or members of your family are members of a particular church and are planning a simple one-day event or banquet, you may want to approach a church leader about the possibility of renting the meeting hall or community room. Very often there is a kitchen adjacent to the hall, used for church events. The price for renting a church hall is usually quite reasonable and the members of your family will be responsible for the set-up and clean up of the facility. It is also a nice gesture to invite the clergy person and his or her spouse to the event gratis, and even to ask him or her to deliver a blessing or benediction.

Hotel - Holding your reunion at a hotel can be a more costly affair. You always want someone on your reunion committee to visit the hotel personally. Never rent space in a hotel unseen! It is imperative that you meet with the hotel sales and catering management, get a full tour of the entire facility, discuss your needs, and negotiate pricing. Here are some considerations you should bear in mind when working with hotels:

- You have leverage! You are bringing business to the hotel and you have choices.
- Meeting rooms may be rented on a per diem basis and, depending on the hotel, the rate may be $200 or more per day. If you have family members coming in from out of town and you can guarantee the hotel a certain number of sleeping rooms, it is not unusual for the hotel to give you the use of the meeting room for free. Always ask what the threshold for sleeping room-to-meeting room ratio might be to entitle you to this freebie. If you have a large reunion and require multiple meeting rooms, it may be possible that you have enough attendees using sleeping rooms to merit your free use of multiple meeting rooms.
- Always ask what comes with a meeting room. You will certainly need tables and chairs, but what tablecloths or draping comes with the tables? If you are using the meeting room for a meeting or presentation, the hotel will set the room up to your specifications. You can tell them to set up rows of chairs in a specific configuration, or to set up tables and chairs in classroom style or in any dining style. In a meeting room type of set-up, a hotel will usually provide glasses and pitchers of ice water at no charge.

- If you are hosting a banquet event, are any centerpieces provided and, if so, do you have a choice? You definitely want to see them. If none are available or supplied, be sure to ask if you can provide your own centerpieces. (Some hotels have florists as tenants and may have contractual arrangements that preclude customers providing their own floral arrangements; you might get stuck paying a premium hotel florist price if you are not careful.) What kind of decorations do you want for your event? Do you want to decorate the banquet room yourself? If so, make sure you clear this with the hotel in advance. Some hotels do not allow decorations in banquet rooms, and others allow them only if hotel personnel can put them up and take them down, which can add to your expense.

- What audio/visual equipment do you need? Does the hotel provide anything as part of the room arrangement? It is not unusual for a hotel to provide an overhead projector, a screen, and/or a flip chart and markers at no additional charge. Do you need a podium? What about a microphone? These can be additional cost items.

- You probably want to arrange for a greeting table in the lobby of the hotel. If you're going to host your entire reunion at a hotel, you will probably want a registration/sign-in table at which family members can check in and pick up any registration materials when they arrive. This may also serve as an information desk for your event. Tell the hotel about this requirement and ask that they provide a table, chairs, and a table cloth or draping for a nice, neat appearance. The hotel should provide these items at no charge.

- If you are hosting your event at a large hotel or if you are staging multiple events at the same time, such as a banquet and a children's party, you will want some type of signage. Depending on the hotel, you may have multiple options available:

  1. Floor signs are usually stand-alone signs with square or rectangular frames into which you insert cardboard signs or sheets of paper.
  2. Easels are great for larger, poster board signs that you would probably make yourself or have made for you.
  3. Press-letter signs are those with horizontal channels into which one presses contrasting colored letters to create a sign.
  4. Electronic signs are used in larger, more sophisticated hotels. These require someone to program the name of your event and its location into a computer and then the event is advertised on a television monitor or an electronic sign board. There is usually a cost associated with this type of signage.
  5. Television signage is programmed into a computer and then transmitted to guest room TVs on the hotel's closed circuit television system. This is great signage for a very large group where there are multiple activities taking place throughout the reunion, but there is usually a cost associated with it.

- Always work with the sales department of the hotel and ask them to provide you with a written proposal detailing all the facilities, products, services, and amenities included in their offering. On receipt of their proposal, compare it carefully with the notes you took while visiting with their representative. If you have any questions or notice any discrepancies, contact the sales representative immediately. Usually these are a case of misunderstanding or miscommunication and can be resolved with a simple telephone call. If there are any changes to be made to the original proposal, request that a revised copy be sent to you.

- Do some comparison-shopping and meet with several hotels. You sometimes can play one hotel against another by sharing some of the higher fees (not the entire proposal!) and allowing one hotel to present a more competitive proposal to you. Never sign a contract with a hotel until you have obtained competitive price quotations from all your candidates.

- Request a formal written contract from your hotel of choice. On receipt, compare it against the proposal to make sure all points are covered and that there are no surprises. Make sure there are two copies of the contract. Sign both and make sure you retain one copy signed by the hotel and yourself for your files.

Resort - A really high-class reunion might be held at some type of resort. When it comes to resorts, there is virtually something for everyone and in every price range. You might consider a family reunion at a dude ranch or ski resort.  Female relatives might opt for a "ladies only" reunion spa where they can be pampered and share girl talk, while males might choose a resort specializing in golf, fishing, or some other outdoor activity.  If you are planning a resort reunion, expect to pay top dollar for many of the amenities, especially sleeping accommodations. Depending on the resort and any specialty it offers, many of the cost components discussed in the hotel section above would apply to the resort as well.

Cruise - A family cruise, like a resort reunion, may be an expensive proposition. However, there are low-cost cruises available and you can often save money by booking a cruise in the off-season.  Your best option in organizing a family reunion cruise is to work through a reliable travel agent. A travel agent can work with you to understand your requirements and can then work with the cruise line to design an optimum package for you based on the number of passengers, their ages, their food requirements, and any special events you would like to arrange. This might include setting aside separate areas of the ship, such as a lounge, a salon, the library, or a cordoned off area of the deck for a private reception or party. Depending on the size of your group, your travel agent will have more leverage than you would in negotiating pricing with the cruise line. Bear in mind that deposits are required in advance and, at some date prior to departure, the deposits become non-refundable. The earlier you begin planning a family reunion cruise, the better the chance of finding the combinations you want at the right price. Also, the larger the number of people you bring to the negotiation table, the better per-person deal your travel agent will be able to arrange for you.

Permits and Licenses

As you are planning your family reunion, don't overlook the need for permits or licenses for certain activities. The fees may seem small but failure to obtain a permit or license may result in a stiff fine. For example, in Chicago, Illinois, you need to obtain a picnic permit in order to have a family picnic or barbecue in the city parks. When you apply for a permit, you must declare the date and location of your picnic. The cost of the permit defrays the city's cleanup and maintenance expense and the granting of the permit helps the city ensure that there are not too many events occurring in a specific park at one time. In Tampa, Florida, many of the parks and forest preserves have

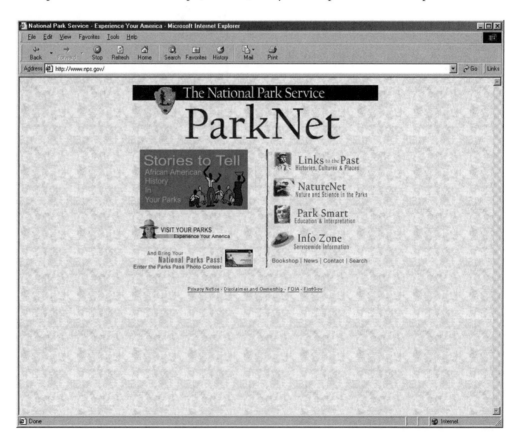

pavilions conducive to group gatherings and you must make arrangements in advance in order to use them. In both cities, there can be fines associated with failure to obtain permits or make advance arrangements. You will want to check with the local governmental offices to determine the rules and fees for using their facilities. You also may find information about these regulations at the city's Web site.

The use and serving of alcoholic beverages may be prohibited in some areas and/or may require a special license, even in some hotels. You would be wise to investigate this question with local authorities; don't always rely on hotel personnel to provide this information. If a license is required, you should factor this cost into your budget.

If you decide to host a family reunion in the form of a camping trip at a national park, you also need to be aware of the fee structure and any permits required. There are 25,700 campsites in 548 campgrounds found at seventy-seven areas of the United States' National Park Service System. You can obtain details at its Web site at <http://www.nps.gov> (opposite), including such things as the need for permits for back-country camping, trailer size restrictions, and other facts. You can even make reservations in advance over the Internet.

Hunting, fishing, and trapping licenses and permits are essential for an outdoorsy family outing. The U.S. Fish & Wildlife Service's Web site at <http://www.fws.gov> provides an excellent starting point for obtaining information about licenses and permits, including links at <http://offices.fws.gov/statelinks.html> to offices in all the states and territories.

Catering and Food Expenses

Everybody has to eat, and most family reunions are planned around meals. Picnics, barbecues and cookouts, breakfasts, luncheons, buffets, banquets, and even pizza parties are all typical meal events. Some meals are traditional while others have themes. Regardless of how large or small your family reunion may be, chances are you'll end up coordinating at least one family meal. Your job is to try to make as many people happy as possible with the meal choices while still maintaining a reasonable budget. Of course, you need to know what kind of crowd you're dealing with. Is it the filet mignon crowd or the tuna salad set? Only you and your committee can make the correct determination.

The type of family reunion you host certainly determines the type of food offered and its expense. If your reunion takes place at someone's home, you may want to consider a covered dish affair with each family bringing one or more dishes to share. On the other hand, your reunion may be such that it makes sense to hire a caterer to prepare and serve the food for you. The difference in cost can be substantial. A covered dish meal entails only the preparer's cost of the ingredients and the preparation time, while a catered meal may cost a bit more depending on the menu selected. When some or many people are coming from substantial distances away, it may be impossible or impractical for them to prepare and bring food to contribute to the reunion. In those cases, you will almost always want to opt for a catered event.

You may want to consider controlling food expenses by combining home-cooked fare with catered food. At one weekend family reunion in their old hometown, a medium-sized family decided to do exactly that. The family members living there took turns hosting breakfasts and lunches, reserving evening meals as more formal occasions. Most family members arrived on Friday afternoon or evening and one family hosted an ongoing buffet at their home throughout the evening. Two other families volunteered to prepare and serve breakfast at their respective homes on Saturday and Sunday mornings. Lunch on Saturday consisted of a barbecue in another family's backyard. Saturday night was reserved for the big catered banquet. As a result, the per-person cost was kept under control because family members' labor was used to host all the meals except the big banquet. The only costs for all the other meals, therefore, were confined to groceries. In the meantime, these other meals provided an opportunity for casual mingling of family members and for the host families to show off their homes.

When working with a caterer, there are some essential rules you should follow. Remember, you are bringing them business, giving you leverage you can use in negotiating with them. Also, remember that the perception of success of the entire reunion may rest on the quality of the food and the impression it leaves on your family. Here are some important rules to keep in mind:

- Do your homework and be prepared with several scenarios before you meet with the caterer.
- Differentiate between adult meals and children's meals. A terrific lunch for children and teenagers might be a selection of pizzas and soft drinks catered by the local pizzeria.

- Have an exact count of the number of people to be fed (or as close as possible). This gives you precise information with which to negotiate, and gives the caterer the information he or she needs to prepare a specific estimate for you. Break this amount down into the number of adults and the number of children. You certainly do not want to pay full adult price for the children's meals. Also, ask the caterer about reduced rates for senior citizens' meals. This may save you some money that, in turn, you can pass on to family members in the form of reduced registration fees.
- Decide in advance how elaborate a meal you would like served. A satisfying luncheon might consist of sliced turkey on a croissant, served with fresh fruit and potato salad, topped off with a fudge brownie for dessert. A dinner selection might consist

of a salad, roast beef or some special chicken dish, served with roasted potatoes, green beans, and dinner rolls, followed by a dessert of cheesecake topped with fresh blueberries or strawberries.

- Ask the caterer to show you specific menu choices. They should have examples from previous catering jobs. Ask for details about the food components, such as what grade of beef is used in the preparation of steaks and roast beef dishes. Ask whether fresh or frozen vegetables, such as green beans and peas, are used.

- Ask about alternate choices and substitutions.

- If you have family members with special dietary needs, make sure you ask the caterer about the availability of meal choices for these relatives.

- Ask to see photographs from previous engagements, and ask for references. Make sure you follow through by making calls to every reference given to you.

- Ask for a detailed written price quotation for every menu choice and be certain that beverages are included. Beverages can become an expensive add-on charge. Make sure that you understand the gratuity rate for your group and request that that amount be included in your written quotation. Tell the caterer that you want a full listing of all charges so there are no surprises. When you receive your quotation, examine it against notes you have taken while you were working with the caterer. Beware of any add-on charges or surprises, and contact the caterer immediately to clear up any misunderstandings. Sometimes it is simply a question of miscommunication or misunderstanding and a non-confrontational discussion can usually clear these up.

- Always get price quotations from more than one caterer. Prices vary substantially from caterer to caterer. You will find that hotel caterers are much more expensive than private catering firms, but negotiating a package deal with a hotel that also includes the use of their catering staff and facilities may ultimately be cheaper for you. I strongly suggest that you speak with no less than four caterers before making a final decision. You may save hundreds of dollars this way.

- Never sign a contract with one caterer until you have all the proposals in hand from all the competitors. The last bid you receive may be the best.

- Request a formal written contract from your caterer of choice. On receipt, compare it against the proposal to make sure all points are covered and that there are no surprises. Make sure there are two copies of the contract. Sign both and make sure you retain one copy signed by the caterer and yourself for your files.

Transportation Expenses

Your family reunion may involve some transportation expenses. These usually fall into two categories:

1. Team members and family volunteers may end up running a number of errands on behalf of the project. Most of these will be short and inexpensive for most people.

However, the errands may add up to a considerable amount of mileage, tolls, and gasoline expense for others. You must decide early whether or not you plan to reimburse anyone for these expenses because it can become a contentious issue. If you plan to reimburse some people and not others, you will want to clearly define the circumstances for reimbursement up front and stick to them.

There are absolutely no IRS guidelines for the use of one's personal automobile for errands run for a family reunion, so don't fall victim to that argument.

2. Your family reunion may include events that involve transportation to and from other locations. These might include an outing to the amusement park for the kids, an excursion to the old family homestead, or a trip to visit the family cemetery. In some cases it may be expedient or desirable to charter buses or passenger vans from a professional transportation company. Here are some points to consider as you're working with these carriers:

- Try to determine in advance how many people will need this type of transportation. This will determine the size of vehicle(s) required. You may find that one or more passenger vans will be sufficient rather than chartering an entire bus.

- Ask about credentials. A professional transportation company will be licensed by the state in which it operates and may also be licensed by the municipality. Ask about the driving record of the person(s) who will be operating the equipment.

- Ask about insurance. It is imperative that the transportation company have ample insurance in the event of an accident. Specifically ask about casualty insurance and liability insurance. In this litigious society, it would not be unusual in the event of an accident for someone to sue the transportation company and the client who hired them, i.e., you.

- Be specific in your discussions about dates, times, pick-up locations, destinations, and any intermediate stops required.

- Request a written proposal containing all fees and any gratuities. On receipt of the proposal, review it carefully against the notes you took. If there are any discrepancies or surprises, contact the company and try to resolve any differences. If there is any change to the original proposal, request a revised proposal.

- Obtain proposals from at least two different companies for review. If you are torn between charter buses and passenger vans, obtain at least two proposals from each type of carrier so you have a base of comparison.

- Request a formal written contract from your transportation company of choice.

On receipt, compare it against the proposal to make sure all points are covered and that there are no surprises. Make sure there are two copies of the contract. Sign both and make sure you retain one copy signed by the company and yourself for your files.

Hired Personnel Expenses

There may be people you wish to hire for specific tasks during your family reunion. Usually these people provide a special skill not found among family members, or you may just want to hire a function out to free yourself or other family members to enjoy the reunion. You will usually engage these people after you have determined the dates and locations of your reunion events. You therefore will already have much of the information required to discuss the reunion in detail and to negotiate with them. Don't wait until the last minute, however, to make arrangements for these individuals. If you do, you may find that the professionals you want are already booked or that you will be unable to negotiate as good a deal as you might have otherwise.

The four most frequently-hired personnel for family reunions are photographers, videographers, disk jockeys (DJs), and children's entertainers. Let's discuss each of these potential employees, as well as some tips for selecting the best talent at the best price.

 **Photographers** - Family reunions present many photo opportunities and, for the most part, family members will take advantage of the chance to take photographs themselves. However, you may decide that a professional photographer could take "official" photographs of the reunion to help guarantee high quality pictures that you and other family members might purchase. The following are some considerations to bear in mind as you are working with potential photographers for your event:

- You can pay anything you want for a photographer. You can hire a professional studio photographer, a photographer who specializes in weddings and similar events, or a freelance photographer. You have to decide on a price range to fit your budget. This will depend to a great degree on what finished product you desire, and what you believe the interest level will be on the part of other family members in purchasing professional photographs.
- Decide what kind of photographs you want before you begin discussions with the photographer. Do you want casual shots and, if so, do you want them taken at a single event, such as a banquet, or throughout the duration the reunion? Do you want portrait shots, such as family group portraits and/or a photograph of the entire family assemblage? By knowing what you want up front and by understanding what people will and will not be interested in purchasing, you can provide the photographer with a better idea of what is

entailed in the job on which he or she is bidding. Some families build professional photographic service into the registration cost, perhaps offering a family portrait and a large reunion group photograph as an optional item. Family members pay the price of the photographs at the time they submit their registration form and that covers the photographer's expense before the reunion. This is an ideal situation, especially since some photographers require deposits or down payments in advance.

- Ask to see representative samples of the photographer's work. Most photographers already have an album or portfolio they are happy to show and to explain specific jobs and photographic techniques. The sample photographs will give you an idea of the quality of the photographer's work.
- Examine individual photograph samples at random, checking the back to determine what brand of photographic paper was used. Some photographers use "off brands" to save money and increase their profit margin. Your reunion photographs are important family keepsakes and you therefore want to make sure the best quality photographic papers and processing materials are used. Be sure you specify to the photographer that you want high quality paper and chemicals used in the developing of your photographs. Kodak brand photographic paper and chemicals are always a safe bet.
- Be prepared to provide the photographer with the dates, times, and location(s) when you wish him or her to provide the service.
- Ask for references from the photographer and follow through by making contact with those people.
- Request a written proposal containing all fees and any gratuities. Upon receipt of the proposal, review it carefully against the notes you took. If there are any discrepancies or surprises, contact the photographer and try to resolve any differences. If there is any change to the original proposal, request that a revised proposal be sent to you.

- Obtain proposals from at least two different photographers offering the same services. Remember that studio photographers, professional wedding photographers, and freelance photographers may offer similar services but, because of different overhead expenses, their pricing may be substantially different. Therefore, it is important to compare the descriptions of their services, the quality of their sample photographs, and their pricing to make sure you are comparing apples with apples.

- Never sign a contract with one photographer until you have all the proposals in hand from all the competitors. The last bid you receive may be the best.
- Request a formal written contract from your photographer of choice. On receipt, compare it against the proposal to make sure all points are covered and that there are no surprises. Make sure there are two copies of the contract. Sign both and retain one copy signed by the photographer and yourself for your files.

Videographers - Many of the same guidelines for photographers also apply to videographers. It is a similar art form but the medium is substantially different. Anyone can operate a video camera; the key is to locate a professional who can both capture the event in a positive manner and produce a high-quality video-tape for posterity. Here are some tips for evaluating and working with videographers.

- Decide what kind of video record you want made of your family reunion. Do you want a video made of a single event, such as a banquet or an amusement park outing? Do you want random moments captured on video throughout the reunion and compiled into a video montage? Or do you want a combination of all of the above?
- Ask to see representative samples of the videographer's work. Most will already have sample videos and will be happy to show and explain specific jobs and video techniques. The samples will give you an idea of the quality of his or her work and may give you additional ideas for the types of videos you would like to have taken and reproduced.
- Be prepared to provide the videographer with the dates, times, and location(s) when you wish him or her to provide the service.
- Ask for references from the videographer and follow through by making contact with those people.
- Request a written proposal containing all fees and any gratuities. On receipt of the proposal, review it carefully against the notes you took. If there are discrepancies or surprises, contact the videographer and try to resolve any differences. If there is any change to the original proposal, request that a revised proposal be sent to you.
- Obtain proposals from at least two videographers offering the same services.
- Request a formal written contract from your videographer of choice. On

receipt, compare it against the proposal to make sure all points are covered and that there are no surprises. Make sure there are two copies of the contract. Sign both and make sure you retain one copy signed by the videographer and yourself for your files.

Disc Jockeys - Music can add a great deal to a family reunion, setting the tone and providing atmosphere. Background music for a banquet adds another dimension and a certain ambience to the occasion. In other cases, you might want to incorporate dancing into your family reunion and make it a real party. Some families have members who are talented in serving as disc jockeys  (or DJs). Most, however, find it preferable to hire someone with the necessary skills, sound equipment, and type of music desired. There are DJs who "spin" all types of music, from big band music of the 1940s up to today's most current hits. If you decide you want to engage a DJ for your family reunion, here are some tips to help you make the right decision:

- Decide in advance what type of music you want for your event. This will immediately help you weed out any DJs who don't provide the type of music you want. Start with telephone calls to any prospective DJs to determine whether they satisfy your musical requirements.
- Next, decide when you want the music performed. That includes the date, location, and specific time periods. A typical evening affair might include background music during a banquet, followed by dancing in whatever style you choose from 8:00 P.M. to 10:00 P.M. By knowing exactly what you want in advance, the DJ can present a proposed program to you.
- Ask the DJ if you can borrow a sample audio tape with representative samples of the music he or she would be using. You can use this tape when discussing selection of the right DJ with your other committee members.
- Make sure the DJ carries his own insurance for accident and injury. In addition, make sure that he or she is responsible for any liability or damage to his or her equipment.
- Request a written proposal containing all fees and any gratuities. Upon receipt of the proposal, review it carefully against the notes you took. Make sure the insurance and liability questions discussed in the previous point are covered in the proposal. If there are any discrepancies or surprises, contact the DJ and try to resolve any differences. If there is any change to the original proposal, request that a revised proposal be sent to you.

- Ask for references from the DJ and follow through by making contact with those people.
- Obtain proposals from at least two different DJs offering the same services.
- Request a formal written contract from your DJ of choice. On receipt, compare it against the proposal to make sure all points are covered and that there are no surprises. Make sure there are two copies of the contract. Sign both and make sure you retain one copy signed by the DJ and yourself for your files.

Children's Entertainers - A family reunion that covers a weekend or longer always requires special planning to ensure that there is something for everyone. Children and teenagers certainly do not enjoy being around grown-ups for extended periods of time. You will want to organize special activities and events specifically geared to the younger set. In the discussion of food earlier in this chapter, I mentioned the possibility of hosting a pizza party for the kids. Special food is a great idea, but you can enhance the experience and prolong the event by providing entertainment.

Children enjoy special entertainers for their events. Depending on the ages of the children, you might want to consider engaging a clown, a magician, or a professional children's entertainer who facilitates games and other activities. As you begin working with these people, you will find that most of them are available at quite reasonable rates. Here are some tips for engaging and negotiating with children's entertainers:

- As with the other professionals discussed previously, it is important to decide up front what type of entertainment you want. This will depend on several factors:
    - The number and ages of the children.
    - The children's interests.
    - The type of event you are staging, e.g., pizza party, games night, costume party, or some other themed event.
    - The duration of the event.
- Be specific about when you want the entertainment. That means knowing the date, location, and exact times of the entertainment. Some children's entertainers are available only during certain times of the day because of their own family obligations. By the same token, you may only want to stage an event for small children during the morning or afternoon hours.
- Don't dictate to the entertainer what they should and should not present. Instead, let them tell you what they have to offer and share with you the benefit of their experiences. They certainly know what works and what doesn't work with a younger audience. They may also have entertainment modules geared toward children who are related.
- Ask the entertainer if he or she has photographs or videos of events they have handled. Also ask for references from past clients. Follow through and make contact with each reference.

• Ask the entertainer about pricing for the entire event package, including whether there are any additional charges for special props used in the entertainment.

• Many children's entertainers today carry liability insurance to cover them in the event of an accident or injury to a child during one of their performances or events. You may want to discuss that with the entertainer and ask him or her to include something in the written proposal. (You will always want responsible family members present during any children's party in case of an accident or emergency.)

• Request a written proposal containing all fees and any gratuities. On receipt of the proposal, review it carefully against the notes you took. If there are any discrepancies or surprises, contact the entertainer and try to resolve any differences. If there is any change to the original proposal, request that a revised proposal be sent to you.

• You may want to obtain at least two proposals from different entertainers so that you have different entertainment scenarios to review and to have a point of comparison for pricing and services.

• Request a formal written contract from your entertainer of choice. On receipt, compare it against the proposal to make sure all points are covered and that there are no surprises. Make sure there are two copies of the contract. Sign both and make sure you retain one copy signed by the entertainer and yourself for your files.

As you can see, there are a number of special considerations you must bear in mind when working with hired professionals. One important key is that you prepare yourself in advance and have a good idea about exactly what you want. It is important to obtain written proposals from every person or company you may potentially hire. You will ultimately want to sign a contract with them for their services. Be wary of anyone who is reluctant to sign such an agreement. A written contract, signed by both parties, is legal protection for both of you in the event of a problem or dispute. The contract will clearly delineate the terms of your relationship, and should include a full description of products and/or services, the description of any liability issues, and a clear statement of your pricing agreement. Whatever you do, don't overlook contracts when dealing with hired professionals.

Decorations and Signage

Depending on the size and type of reunion you host, there are two expense areas that you may want to consider: decorations and signage. Decorations can make a distinct impression on the attendees and add a gala atmosphere to the occasion. For a larger reunion or one with multiple events, such as a reunion weekend held in a hotel or resort, the use of signage to help direct people and provide information can be invaluable. Both decorations and signage come at a cost, and the cost considerations should be taken into account as you develop your budget. You will want someone to take responsibility for managing these items for your reunion. Let's discuss each item separately.

Decorations - Decorations come in all shapes, sizes, and varieties. Alone or in combination, balloons, streamers and bunting, ribbons and bows, party favors, flowers and table centerpieces add a festive and celebratory touch to any occasion. Decorations for your reunion are no different.

The decorations chosen for any occasion, including a family reunion, should be planned with some care. If you include a children's party in your family reunion celebrations, you might want to consider using crepe-paper streamers in the party area to add a festive touch. For a banquet, you might want to consider using a floral centerpiece on each table and perhaps a larger floral arrangement in front of the speaker's podium. While the possibilities are endless, here are some examples of decorations used at family reunions for which you would want to develop financial estimates for use in your budget:

- **Floral arrangements** - Floral pieces are typically used as table centerpieces and as accents in special areas.
- **Streamers** - Crepe paper streamers are a popular form of decoration. They are available in a wide variety of colors and widths and can provide a custom look when strung across a room, over tables or a dance floor, or used as scallop trim on tables and chairs.
- **Ribbons and bows** - More costly than crepe paper, but more elegant, are ribbons and bows. Also available in a wide variety of colors, textures, and widths, ribbon ware can provide a stunning decorative effect.
- **Bunting** - Most of us are familiar with bunting in the form of red, white, and blue fabric swags used at Fourth of July events. However, fabric bunting or swags can be used for elegant decorations in a variety of motifs. Decorative accent bunting placed around the edges of dining tables, on a podium, across the tops of windows, and across easels and poster boards can create a color-coordinated effect for an entire room. Punctuated with coordinated ribbons and/or bows, the effect can be stunning.
- **Candles** - Candles can be used as stand-alone centerpieces or in conjunction with flowers, reflective foil-and-wire decorations, and with other non-flammable materials.
- **Party favors** - Complimentary party favors can add a terrific touch to any reunion event. These can take a variety of forms:
  - Match books imprinted with the family surname
  - Cocktail napkins imprinted with the family surname
  - Party horns and party hats color-coordinated with other decorations and/or imprinted with the family surname
  - The options really are limitless!

- **Poster boards and other family displays** - You may want to create family decorations using poster boards or display tables. Posters may be placed on easels during specific events, mounted on the wall, or simply propped up on tables. If one or more of your family members is involved in family history research, displays of pedigree charts, family group sheets, and other documents might be appropriate. These are great items to generate interest in expanding one's knowledge of the family history. Other displays might include family artifacts, examples of handwork (quilting, knitting, crocheting, tatting and embroidery), family Bibles and other treasured family possessions. In these cases, the only expenses involved may be for poster boards and mounting materials.

Signage - The use of signs can be an effective means of communication with family members at a reunion. If your reunion is a simple family picnic gathering in a park, signs are important to provide directions to the right place. In a hotel or resort where there may be multiple events in different places, you will certainly need to use signs to direct people to the right places at the right times. Signs can take a variety of forms as we discussed earlier in this chapter when we discussed hotels. Electronic signage provided by a hotel may cost money so be certain you discuss this with the hotel sales representative. Other signage that you might provide should also be included in your budget. Here are some examples of signage you might use:

- **Banners** - Banners can add a dynamic, personalized look and feel to the event. You might consider a welcome banner or one stating your family name and the dates of the reunion, as in "Morgan Family Reunion - February 1-4, 2001 - Key West, FL." A 3 ft. by 10 ft. custom banner made of laminated canvas will cost about $125. Other materials can be used that are available at different prices. A paper banner may be substantially cheaper. Shop around for the right material at the right price to meet your budget.
- **Poster board sign**s - You can have poster-sized signs mounted on easels in various places. You can make these yourself or have a printing company make them for you at a fairly reasonable price. Determine in advance how many poster board signs you require and where you want to place them. For instance, you might want directional signs in a hotel lobby or corridor pointing people to specific activities or events. You might want a sign outside a banquet room stating "Smith Family Reunion Banquet - 8:00 P.M. Tonight!" Determine how many signs you need, develop the cost information, and include this in your budget.
- **Small signs** - You may not need large signs at all. Smaller ones may suffice, including ones that can be inserted into freestanding sign posts in hotel lobbies. These sign posts typically consist of a pedestal on top of which is a picture frame-like receptacle into which your sign may be inserted. While hotels usually provide these free of charge, be sure to ask your hotel representative

during your negotiations about the use of the signposts. If there is a cost, you will need to add that to your budget. Consider creating signs and banners on a computer and printing them. This can usually be easily done and can save some expense.

Commemorative Clothing and Other Items

It is very popular these days to distribute commemorative clothing or other mementoes at family reunions. You can get almost any piece of clothing customized, and there are hundreds of Internet-based companies available to help you choose just the right item. Among the most popular pieces of clothing used for this purpose are T-shirts, baseball caps, visors, sweatshirts, sweatbands, fanny packs, and windbreaker jackets.

There are other sports items customized and used to commemorate family reunions. These include baseballs, footballs of all sizes, Nerf balls, tennis balls, and golf balls and tees.

If you're looking for other commemorative items, you might consider coffee mugs, paper weights, key rings, bumper stickers, pens and pencils, lapel buttons and pens, picture frames, notebooks and address books, and a wealth of other promotional items.

You can locate promotional vendors dealing in these types of items by consulting your telephone yellow pages

Don't be reluctant to ask for samples of the items to which you've narrowed your choices. Some vendors will be able to order samples for you to examine; others may only be able to provide you with a photograph.

For Your Information

under a heading like "advertising specialties." There are also hundreds of such vendors on the Internet. Some of the best resources for commemorative merchandise for family reunions are listed at the end of this chapter.

Don't be reluctant to ask for samples of the items to which you've narrowed your choices. Some vendors will be able to order samples for you to examine; others may only be able to provide you with a photograph. Since some merchandise is manufactured overseas, it is wise to provide as much lead-time as possible when placing your order.

As with other resources we've discussed so far, you will want to obtain a written proposal or estimate from the promotional vendor. The proposal should include the cost for the merchandise itself, any graphics set-up charges, any special packaging or wrapping charges, and shipping, handling, and insurance fees. On receipt of the proposal, review it against the notes you took when you worked with the vendor. If there are any discrepancies, contact the vendor as soon as possible to resolve them. Request a revised proposal if necessary. When you sign the order, you are then committed to take delivery of the merchandise when it arrives and to pay for it.

One thing to keep in mind is that some reunion committees choose to let family members know about commemorative items in the registration package. They describe the commemorative pieces, such as wearing apparel, sports equipment, or other materials, and let them know they will be distributed at the reunion. They may request that people order specific quantities and sizes and make full or partial payment at that time.

This is a great approach because it brings in the money to pay for the merchandise early and reduces the need for up-front seed money to perhaps finance the purchase of the merchandise months in advance of the actual reunion.

Supplies and Equipment

One of the biggest expenses of any reunion can be in the area of supplies and equipment. When you consider the cost of office supplies such as paper, envelopes, checkbook and checks, stamps, pens and pencils, labels, a stapler and staples, paper clips, rubber bands, file folders, nametags, shipping labels, binders and other items, the expenses begin to add up. You should do your best to try to budget for these items early in the planning process.

One of the things we will discuss in this and later chapters concerns record-keeping systems. The person acting as treasurer will probably need a good accounting program, such as *Quicken*, to track income and expenditures and to write checks. Another person, perhaps acting as secretary, may be responsible for building and maintaining a database of family contact names and addresses and for tracking registrations. He or she will probably need some sort of software as well. Therefore, as part of your supplies and equipment budget, you should anticipate the purchase of software to automate these processes. If you are lucky, one of your team members may already have a copy of the software installed on his or her computer system and has some experience and expertise in working with it. Otherwise, be prepared to do some comparison-shopping at computer, software, and/or office supply stores for the best deal for the software package.

Don't forget to check the Internet for the software companies that manufacture the packages you want. You can get details at their Web sites and can sometimes download demo versions of the software so you can try them out before you buy. In addition, there are several Web sites where you can find freeware or shareware software packages that may provide all the functionality you need for little or no money. Two of the best sites for this purpose are TuCows at <http://www.tucows.com> and Download.com at <http://www.download.com>. You can search at both sites for accounting or money management software for the financial end of your reunion and database software for the registration and family contact information.

Developing a Realistic Budget

So far in this chapter we have discussed all the major cost components of a family reunion. There are probably other items that could be included as well, things that are unique to your own reunion. What is important, however, is that you develop a realistic budget for your event. The operative word here is *realistic*. This means that you and your reunion team have to do your advance research thoroughly and gather as much information as possible.

In its simplest form, your budget will consist of the following items:

1. Categories of expense items with each component item listed with a realistic estimate of what it will cost.

Family Reunion Budget Spreadsheet

DESCRIPTION/VENDOR	UNIT DESCRIPTION		UNIT PRICE	EXTENSION
Telephone calls	Estimated 50 calls		$3.00	$150.00
Paper (reams)		6	7.50	45.00
Envelopes (cases)		8	11.00	88.00
Postage for mailings	45 families x 5 mailings		0.34	76.50
Hotel meeting room	Gardenia Room		250.00	250.00
Catering for banquet	Children & senior meals x 28		8.75	245.00
Catering for banquet	Adult meals x 72		11.00	792.00
T-shirts Galore!	Commemorative T-shirts		7.50	750.00
Supplies & equipment	Various		350.00	350.00
Accounting software	Quicken		85.00	85.00
Rockin' Robbie	Disk jockey		125.00	125.00
Pretty Flowers, Inc.	20 centerpieces for banquet		15.00	300.00
Julian's Party Supplies	Decorations		100.00	100.00
Photo Phil's Photography	Photography at banquet		75.00	75.00
				$3,431.50

Take $3,431.50 and subtract the meal figures of $245.00 and $792.00, leaving $2,394.50.
This model assumes an attendance of 100 people, 28 of whom are children or seniors.
Divide $2394.50 by 100—a price of $23.95 per person—and add the per person meal
price to this figure. Your per person prices, excluding any optional activities, are as follows:

Adults:	**$34.95**
Children and seniors:	**$32.70**

2. Categories of income items with each component listed with a realistic estimate what the income will be.

Your basic goal is to break even. In some circumstances, your goal may be to make some small profit that will become the seed money for the next reunion. Most important of all, however, is to develop a thorough budget that includes every single component you can think of. Anything that you omit or miscalculate can cause you a problem later. In the worst case scenario, you may have to go back to family members and ask them for more money to cover any shortage. That can be embarrassing. Therefore, I suggest that for your first reunion you add in a contingency or "fudge factor" of at least 10 percent. If you don't use the money for this reunion, it can be set aside for the next reunion or refunded back to family members.

In the previous chapter, we talked about building a team with core members and committees assigned specific responsibilities. Throughout this chapter, we've discussed categories of expenses and examined individual components and their costs. In order to develop a realistic budget, everyone involved in the planning and organization needs to get started with their respective area. This means brainstorming and planning the content in their area and making decisions on what will and will not be included. The next step for some people is to start making contact with hotels, caterers, potential hired personnel, transportation companies, and vendors of commemorative apparel and other materials. For others, this means investigating the cost of flowers, decorations, signage materials, supplies and equipment, or any permits or licenses required. After everyone has conducted their research and/or made contact with vendors, each responsible person or committee should compile their figures into some format for presentation to the treasurer. At that juncture, the treasurer can start compiling a budget listing all the expenses for the reunion. At the conclusion of this exercise, you should have a budget to review.

Your next step is to study each category of the budget and its component items to ensure that you haven't missed something. Examine the cost for each component item and review the committees' notes and any proposals received from vendors. Scrutinize the proposals to ensure that you are comparing apples with apples, and then compare the proposed costs. Weigh the recommendations and comments from references provided by the vendors. It is probably at this point that you begin making the hard decisions about which proposals you accept and which ones you reject.

Your review of the budget cost figures may astonish or overwhelm you. Now you must make an estimate based on your family survey to determine how many people will attend the family reunion. Take the total cost figure for the reunion and divide it by the number of people you expect to attend the event. At this point, you now have your first look at the per-person registration fee. Is it too high? Will some people balk at the fee? Now is the time to go back and re-examine the component costs. You may now need to delete some frill items and/or scale back on others to make the registration fee more attractive to family members.

Next, you need to look at sources of income to offset the costs of the reunion. There are many ways to raise money to pay for the reunion. Consider the following:

- Registration fees are the primary source of income for family reunions. They will offset the majority of the hotel meeting room expenses, catering and food expenses, permits and license fees, hired personnel expenses, decorations and signage, supplies and equipment, and other incidentals.
- Additional fees may be collected from registrants for special add-on, optional items. These might include the sale of photographs taken by the professional photographer, commemorative clothing and other items, transportation to and from optional events, and admission fees for optional events.
- Special one-time contributions from family members intended to get the reunion off to a good start.
- Fundraisers staged by family members for the purpose of helping fund the reunion, such as bake sales, car washes, or baby-sitting.
- Publication of the family newsletter for the event in which local businesses are solicited to place ads for a small fee.
- Use your imagination to develop additional fundraising ideas to help finance your reunion.

At this point, you should have a pretty strong idea of what the reunion is going to cost the family. You should also have a good understanding of what you are going to have to charge family members in the way of registration fees. It is now that you set the registration rate.

Registration Fees

Your registration fees will be a key item in the decision-making process for potential attendees. If the fees are too high, people may decide not to come. One approach used by many families involves setting registration rates based on the age of the attendee. In this scenario, adults pay full price while children under twelve years of age and senior citizens over age sixty-five are charged a reduced registration fee. Babies should usually be free. If, in the course of your negotiations with the caterer, you were able to negotiate a lower rate for children's and seniors' meals, this savings may help you justify a reduced registration fee for them. Such discounts also encourage families with children and senior citizens with limited incomes to attend the event.

Building an Effective Record-Keeping System

We're almost there with the finances! So far we have discussed categories of cost items and the components of each of the categories. We have looked at developing a budget using those costs and methods for offsetting the costs with income items. We also listed some key areas concerning how to generate income.

The development of a realistic budget is of paramount importance in the planning and organization of a successful family reunion. You now need to provide your treasurer with the tools to do his or her job. There are several of these:

- First, your treasurer should be using a computer and be conversant with the use of several software programs. An accounting software package for the computer is essential. As mentioned before, a good accounting software program like *Quicken* or one of the freeware or shareware programs available for download at Web sites such as TuCows and Download.com should work nicely.
- A bank account dedicated specifically to the reunion finances is also essential. You do not want reunion money mixed with anyone's personal finances. You will want to open a separate checking account for the reunion and arrange for your treasurer and at least one backup person to have authority to sign checks and deposit or withdraw money.
- Develop a procedure early on regarding reimbursements for personal expenses. This may include the use of expense account forms that individuals complete and to which they attach receipts in order to be reimbursed. For example, if cousin Edith purchases crepe paper for decorations and cellophane tape to put it up, she might submit an expense account form detailing her expenditures and attach her receipts. The treasurer would need to understand what was purchased

so that he or she could allocate the crepe paper purchase to the decorations account category and the cellophane tape purchase to the office supplies account category. At that time, a check can be written by the treasurer to reimburse Cousin Edith.

Your treasurer should set up a filing system based on the categories of expenses and income. He or she would process expenses and write checks on a regular basis, record them in the accounting software program, and file any pertinent documents in the filing system. At the same time, the treasurer would process any income and receipts (such as registration fees), prepare and make bank deposits, record transactions in the accounting software program, and file any documents in the filing system and/or forward them to whoever is handling the record-keeping system for reunion registrations. (We will discuss that record-keeping system in the next chapter.)

The treasurer should prepare accounting reports on a regular basis and review them with the reunion chairperson and other team members as appropriate. People responsible for specific areas should probably see reports for the expenses and income in their own areas so they are aware of their progress against their budget. It is essential to establish a schedule to review finances and stick with it. You want to know as early as possible if there are problems with cash flow, unexpected expenses, and overages so that you can address them quickly.

As you can see, money matters! There are many details to be attended to as you and your team develop a budget and manage the financial affairs of your family reunion. A talented treasurer or financial manager is essential, and the person(s) who might accept the responsibility will have a substantial task ahead of him or her. When the time comes to recognize the contributions of the people who really make a reunion happen, the financial people are often overlooked when, in fact, they are among the most important players on your reunion team. Make sure you give credit where credit is due!

Questions to Ask Yourself

- Based on the type of reunion we are planning, what are all the categories of expenses we must consider?

- What are the component items and costs in each expense category?

- Who will work with the various vendors?

- Have we gotten multiple written proposals to evaluate competitive prices?

- Do we have a signed contract with the vendors whose services we have selected?

- Have we set a registration fee that will adequately cover our expenses? Does it include any discounted fees?

- What kind of record-keeping systems will we use, and who will maintain them?

Internet Resources

To Help You Locate and Purchase Office Supplies, Printers, Hotels, Caterers and Other Vendors

Mailing Materials, Copies, and Postage

- Franklin's Printing – http://www.franklins-printing.com
- Kinko's – http://www.kinkos.com
- Mail Boxes Etc. – http://www.mbe.com
- Office Depot – http://www.officedepot.com
- OfficeMax – http://www.officemax.com
- Staples – http://www.staples.com/
- United States Postal Service – http://www.usps.com (Great site for locating ZIP codes and checking postal rates)

Hotels

- GORP Places to Stay – http://gorp.worldres.com
- HotelsTravel.com – http://www.hotelstravel.com
- Hotels, Resorts, and Inns – http://hotels.about.com/travel/hotels

Caterers

- Leading Caterers of America – http://www.leadingcaterers.com
- Caterers – How to Find and Use One – http://entertaining.about.com/style/entertaining/cs/caterers1

Photographers and Videographers

- Professional Photographers of America – http://www.ppa.com
- Wedding and Event Videographers Association International – http://www.weva.com

Florists

- FTD – http://www.ftd.com
- Teleflora – http://www.afs.com

Commemorative Clothing and Other Items

See Appendix A for suggestions on how to locate advertising specialty vendors using Internet search engines.

Nielsen Family Reunion, 1996

Chapter 4

Record-Keeping Systems

Information is power, and this is emphatically true when it comes to family reunions. Throughout the reunion process, you will be gathering and organizing information about your family. Your starting point may be your own or some other family member's telephone and address book containing names, addresses, telephone numbers, and other contact information. You will certainly use this information as you begin your reunion process and send out the survey questionnaire.

You will want to keep track of every mailing you make to every individual. As surveys and family contact forms are returned, information about family members will start piling up and will need to be recorded somewhere. Corrections to names, addresses, and telephone numbers are common. So are the addi-

In This Chapter ✔

- Types of information you need to compile

- Record-keeping systems that can help manage the information

- Software resources for record keeping

- Internet resources to help you locate record-keeping software and other materials

tions of new family members' names and birth dates, such as for new spouses, children, and grandchildren. The addition of e-mail addresses expands the range of communication possibilities as well. All of these changes and additions will need to be recorded.

The registration process creates the need for additional record keeping for other types of information, such as who is coming to the reunion, who has and hasn't paid their registration fees, who wants how many and what size of commemorative T-shirts, who will attend the banquet, who has special dietary restrictions, who is going to the amusement park and requires transportation, and a myriad of other details. Meticulous attention needs to be paid to the keeping of records for registration.

One of the biggest mistakes made by family reunion organizers is making the record-keeping system too complicated. When it is too big and involved, it becomes cumbersome to work with and the users become frustrated.

In this chapter, we'll discuss the types of record keeping that usually are necessary for every family reunion. Depending on how large your reunion is, where it is held, and the activities you plan, the amount and type of information you need to record in your record-keeping system may be relatively simple or more complex. We'll talk about record-keeping needs in both types of scenarios and provide you with samples. Then we will discuss types of record-keeping systems, both manual and computerized, to help you organize all that information so that it can be readily accessed.

Types of Information

Let's begin by discussing the different types of information you will need to compile, record, and work with during the process of organizing and hosting a family reunion. Information will fall into a number of different categories:

- Family contact information
- Records of every mailing
- Registration records
- Financial information
- Food and meal information

- Orders for commemorative clothing and other materials
- Special events and transportation
- Thank you letters and special recognition

Each category will have its own special informational requirements. Let's begin by describing each of these categories and the types of data typically compiled in a record-keeping system for each one.

Family Contact Information - Communication with other family members is key throughout the reunion organization and planning process. This cannot be stressed enough. We presented the Family Contact Form when we discussed the survey to determine the level of interest in a family reunion. The information you gather about family members can be used in many ways. You might, for instance, consider compiling a family contact address book for distribution at or after the family reunion. (Some families create and sell a family address book as a means of deferring the costs for the book itself and/or as a fundraiser for the next reunion.)

The Family Contact Form (opposite, and in Appendix B) provides a template for your own information-gathering activities. You ultimately will want to have a completed form for every family unit, including single persons, couples, and families. The information you compile will include the following:

- **Title of the primary respondent** - Provide the options for Mr., Mrs., Miss, Ms., Dr., Rev., or other title.
- **Name of the primary respondent** - This should be organized by last name, first name, and middle initial (or middle name, if desired).
- **Address information** - It is recommended that you provide two address lines with space for street address, city, state (or Province), and Postal Code.
- **Birth date of the primary respondent** - You may want to specify the format in which you would like the birth date written. You may want month, day,

Family Contact Sheet

Mr./Mrs./Miss/Ms./Dr./Other: _____

Last Name: _____ First Name: _____ MI: ____

Address #1: _____

Address #2: _____

Apt. # or Mail Drop : _____ Other Designation: _____

City: _____ State: _____ ZIP: _____-_____

Birth date: _____

Home Phone: (_____) _____-_____ Work Phone: (_____) _____-_____

Cellular Phone: (_____) _____-_____

E-mail Address: _____@_____

Web site: http://_____

Spouse's Name: _____ Birthdate: _____

E-mail Address: _____@_____

Children:

Name_____ Birthdate: _____

   E-mail Address: _____@_____

Name_____ Birthdate: _____

   E-mail Address: _____@_____

Name_____ Birthdate: _____

   E-mail Address: _____@_____

Name_____ Birthdate: _____

   E-mail Address: _____@_____

year or the date, month, year or MM/DD/YY or MM/DD/YYYY or DD/MM/YY or DD/MM/YYYY. It all depends on what you want, but be prepared for people not to follow instructions and to enter dates in a variety of formats—usually the format to which they are most accustomed.

- **Telephone numbers** - You will want to pay special attention to telephone numbers. With the addition of new area codes and the changes being made to existing telephone numbers these days, this is a very volatile piece of information. Also, individual family members are increasingly obtaining a variety of telephone numbers. At a minimum, you want to obtain the home telephone number for every person. You may also want to request each person's work and cellular telephone numbers. If a fax number is available, you may want to request that as well.

- **E-mail address** - The proliferation of the Internet and e-mail over the last decade means that the majority of people have one or more e-mail addresses. Since e-mail is an inexpensive means of communication, you will want to obtain people's primary e-mail addresses and use them in many instances.

- **Spouse's name** - You want to be particularly careful to obtain the name of the spouse. The primary respondent may have married, or may have divorced and remarried, since the last time anyone had contact with him or her. It can be embarrassing to compile a family contact list with the wrong spouse name. Worse still, imagine having a nametag in the registration envelope when the family arrives at the reunion that has the name of the previous spouse!

- **Spouse's birth date** - See notes above regarding birth date entries.

- **Spouse's e-mail address** - See note above regarding e-mail addresses.

- **Children's information** - The Family Contact Form found in Appendix B is formatted with the idea that the children are living at home with their parents. This is not always the case. Children of parents who are separated or divorced may be living with another parent. Children away at school may have another mailing address. You want to keep this in mind in developing your own family contact document. In the meantime, the information you probably want includes each child's name and birth date, as well as an e-mail address if they have one.

A record-keeping system for family contact information can be as simple or as elaborate as you would like to make it. A simple system you devise might be to set up file folders lettered A through Z. As contact sheets are returned, they can be filed under

their respective letter of the alphabet. Later, you may decide you want to compile family members' information into an address book. At that time simply take each folder, organize the sheets alphabetically by surname, and transcribe the information into a word processing document for printing, photocopying, and binding.

You could create a more sophisticated record-keeping system by computerizing the information you receive. You might decide to enter the information into a spreadsheet program, defining columns for specific information. When you want to print a report or create a family address book, the spreadsheet program will allow you to sort and re-sequence information, as well as to add formatting to enhance its appearance. Another option might be the use of a computerized database program, such as Microsoft *Access*™, *FoxPro*™ or others. Database programs allow you to define a structured format for the entry and storage of data. Some even use a "wizard" feature to walk you through set-ting up a database. Initially you define fields into which data is entered. Later, the data-base allows you to query or search it and to format and print custom reports using the data that was entered into the system.

Mailing Records - You want to keep track of every mailing to every individual. Earlier in the book, I men-tioned that you will generally make multiple mailings to family members regarding the reunion. We will discuss communications in substantial detail in a Chapter 6. However, it is important to keep track of what materials you have mailed and to whom, and also what you have received back from each person. An example here might illustrate the point.

Perhaps you mailed a survey and a family contact sheet to Cousin Peter, and he com-pleted and returned both of them to you. Your next mailing to him would be an invi-tation to the reunion and a registration form. Let's say he completes and returns the registration form with his check. If you decide to do a final mailing to everyone regis-tered as a reminder of the dates (and to hype the event), you will mail one of these reminders to your Cousin Peter.

In the meantime, your Cousin Peter talks with his sister Penny, and she is interested and excited about attending the reunion, too. Perhaps she calls you and asks for infor-mation about the reunion and you find at that point that she has divorced, remarried, and moved to a new address. You may have already mailed the survey and a family con-tact sheet to her but somehow it was misdirected by the post office and not returned to you. You now have to figure out what to mail to your Cousin Penny. By this time, you already know you're going to have the reunion, so it doesn't make sense to mail the survey. However, you want to send her a registration packet and the family contact sheet. Perhaps, as the reunion date is approaching, you haven't heard anything back from Cousin Penny. At that point, you may want to follow up with a reminder mailing. The reminder may do the trick and you may get a registration form from your cousin but you may not receive a completed family contact sheet. What do you do now? You know you want as complete a contact list as possible for the entire family, so you telephone, send a reminder postcard, or write an e-mail to ask her to complete and return the fam-ily contact sheet.

Family Reunion Mailing Tracking Log

as of 10/1/2000

NAME	SURVEY	REC'D	ANNOUNCE	CONTACT	REC'D	F/U	REG. PKG.	REC'D	F/U	REMINDER
Alexander, John M.	5/10	5/22	6/19	5/10	5/22		6/20	7/1		9/2
DeJournette, Florence			6/19	6/20	7/15		6/20	7/15		9/2
Holder, Edward E.	5/10	5/30	6/19	5/10	5/30		6/20	7/3		9/2
Holder, Green Berry	5/18	6/3	6/19	5/18	6/3		6/20	6/27		9/2
Morgan, John Allen	5/10	5/21	6/19	5/10		7/1	6/20	8/18	8/1	9/2
Morgan, Samuel T.	5/10	5/29	6/19	5/10	5/29		6/20	8/7	8/1	9/2
Morgan, William R.	5/10		6/19	5/10	7/10	7/1	6/20	6/30		9/2
Smith, Andrew M.	5/10	6/1	6/19	5/10	6/1		6/20	6/30		9/2
Weatherly, Martin			6/19	7/1	7/15		6/20	7/11		9/2
Weatherly, Walton C.	5/10	5/22	6/19	5/10	5/22		6/20	7/22		9/2

As you can see, keeping track of who has been mailed what materials and what, if anything, they have returned to you is important. Preparing a simple flowchart for yourself and developing an organizational system can help you manage the entire communication process.

Your tracking system for mailings can be as simple as a checklist. In the left-hand column you might have a list of all the names of family members to whom you have mailed materials. In other columns you may specify Mailing #1, Mailing #2, and so on, and you may enter the date on which the mailing was made. For mailings requiring a response from the recipient, you might add columns for follow-up dates and dates of receipt.

The Family Reunion Message Tracking Log above (also included in Appendix B of this book) was created using the Microsoft *Excel*™ spreadsheet program. It includes columns for name, the date on which a survey was mailed, the date on which the completed survey was received, the date of the reunion announcement's mailing, the date that a contact sheet was mailed as well as its receipt and follow-up (F/U) dates, the date of the mailing of the registration package and its receipt and follow-up dates, and the date of the mailing of the final reunion reminder. Your tracking does not have to be computerized; it may be a simple list in a spiral notebook or on a legal pad. Use what works for you.

Registration Records - Perhaps the most complicated of the record-keeping systems involves registration for the reunion. Registration typically encompasses a number of things:

- Names and contact information for people registering to attend the reunion
- Personal checks, money orders, or other forms of payment
- Designation of events or activities in which individuals will participate (ban-

quet, excursions, and other choices you might offer)
- Special dietary requests
- Orders for commemorative clothing or other merchandise

As a result, different pieces of information may need to be disseminated to different people or committees on your team. For example, the person responsible for keeping record of who has registered for the reunion will need a complete list of persons and their ages. The individual making arrangements for a banquet would need to know the total number of attendees in order to plan seating arrangements and decorations. The person responsible for planning food and catering would need to have a count of adults, children, and seniors, as well as any special dietary needs, as he or she is working with the caterer. Someone responsible for entertainment for the children would need to know how many children will attend and their ages. The treasurer would need a copy of the registration form and the payment so that he or she can keep records and make deposits into the bank account. And the person responsible for ordering commemorative T-shirts would need to know how many of each size to order for the event. As you can see, information gathered from registration forms can be considerable and will need to be disseminated to the right people in order for them to fulfill their responsibilities.

> A simple record-keeping system for registrations might be coupled with the mailing tracking log discussed previously. The tracking log can tell you at a glance who has received the mailing packets and who has responded, so follow-ups can be done.
>
> **For Your Information** ⓘ

A simple record-keeping system for registrations might be coupled with the mailing tracking log discussed previously. The tracking log can tell you at a glance who has received the mailing packets and who has responded, so that follow-ups can be done. In addition, incoming registration forms can be copied and copies can be distributed to all parties who need the information. They, in turn, can devise their own methods for working with the information they receive.

A more elaborate record-keeping system might be created that uses spreadsheet or database programs. Data can be entered as registration forms and payments are received and custom reports can be generated. The primary drawbacks of these types of systems are that A) you need a computer-savvy individual who understands the programs in order to set them up and maintain them, B) you need someone to perform the data-entry activities, and C) you must establish and maintain a schedule for reports to be created for the people who need them. Except for very large reunions involving hundreds of people, elaborate, computerized record-keeping systems are probably overkill. The software can be expensive, and designing, programming, and maintaining them requires a significant time commitment on the part of the programmer and/or administrator.

Financial Records - We discussed finances in the last chapter and touched on the topic of financial record keeping. You already know how crucial it is to keep good financial records; invariably there will be one or more family members who will want to review them.

The system you and your treasurer devise for keeping track of finances should be a relatively simple one. At the outset of the project, when you define categories of income and expenses and their components, you are already setting the stage for the accounting categories to be used by your treasurer. It is a good idea to purchase an accounting software program such as *Quicken* for your treasurer to use on his or her computer. *Quicken*, for example, allows you to define categories and subcategories for both income and expense. When a deposit is made or a check is written, the user can add a description to the transaction as well as associate the transaction with a specific account, category or subcategory. The program provides strong reconciliation and balancing tools as well as robust reporting facilities. Therefore, once the set-up work is accomplished, your treasurer can perform data entry functions and the software program handles the calculations and facilitates reporting for you.

Some families make the mistake of trying to use a spreadsheet program to create an accounting system. While this seems to be an economical approach, in the long run it can be more time-consuming and expensive. A simple accounting program like *Quicken* or those freeware or shareware programs available at TuCows and Download.com will always be your best bet.

Your treasurer will also need to maintain a filing system. You can purchase a simple plastic file box at any office supply store that satisfies this need. The treasurer can create file folders for each income and expense category and subcategory and file the papers, invoices, receipts, expense statements, bank statements, cancelled checks, and copies of accounting reports accordingly. This simple filing system will make it easy to immediately locate any document.

In addition, consider creating a small binder to hold your copies of the contracts you negotiate with the hotel, caterer, and other vendors. Your treasurer should have this binder at his or her fingertips in order to confirm the contract details when invoices arrive.

Food and Meal Information - One of the challenges for the individual or committee working with the caterer or other food service is to keep track of who wants what food. Meal planning is a very important component of organizing a family reunion. Since everyone must eat, you may need to make arrangements for three distinct meals each day. Some families organize breakfasts while others make breakfast an optional or on-your-own meal. Other meals, however, must be planned.

At a simple family reunion, such as a barbecue cookout or picnic, organizing a meal may be a comparatively simple task. It may only involve making contact with family members and asking them to bring a portion of a meal. The difficulty in coordinating

> Some families make the mistake of trying to use a spreadsheet program to create an accounting system. While seemingly economical, in the long run it can be more time consuming and expensive. A simple accounting program will always be your best bet.
>
> **For Your Information**

this type of meal comes with trying to avoid duplication of courses. You certainly don't want nine bowls of potato salad, twelve bags of chips and six jars of dill pickles—and no fried chicken, tossed salad, and desserts! A good system for keeping track of dishes for this kind of food event is to simply start a list. Define the categories for a balanced menu and list specific dishes under each category. People can sign up to bring specific dishes or offer to prepare special family recipes in the various categories. Often you will find family members asking the question, "What should I bring?" You then have a list to refer to and can make suggestions on needed items. Don't forget to suggest such essentials as paper plates, paper cups, cutlery, napkins, and other supplies.

Perhaps the most complicated type of meal event to organize and coordinate is a formal banquet. Many families, as part of their hotel or resort reunion, choose to have a large family dinner, and regardless of whether it is a formal catered affair or a family-style, sit-down dinner, there can be a lot of information to coordinate. These items include:

- **Number of attendees and ages** - Catered dinners, as we have discussed, may be negotiable based on the number of diners and the type of meals served. Therefore, you will need to keep track of how many persons—adults, children, and seniors—will be dining. This final information will need to be communicated to the caterer some time before the event to ensure that the correct numbers and types of meals are prepared.
- **Selection of entrée** - If you offer a choice of entrée, you will need to keep track of who ordered what so the final count can be communicated to the caterer.
- **Special dietary requirements** - Some of your family members may have special dietary needs. One person may be on a sodium-free diet, another on a sugar-free diet, one on a low- or no-fat regimen, and others may prefer vegetarian fare. You certainly want to make these options available to your family members, otherwise they may not come to the reunion at all. But you must be prepared to keep track of how many of each type of special dietary need and who needs it so you can communicate that to the caterer.

Once you have decided on the meal functions and what they will entail, it should be a simple matter to create a record-keeping system to track the information. A simple list, by event, that lists the names of all attendees, their choice of entrée (if there is a choice), and any special dietary needs should be sufficient.

Orders for Commemorative Clothing and Other Materials - Commemorative items such as the ones we have already discussed become treasured mementoes of a family reunion. Each time they are seen or used, they will bring back memories of a unique and special event. It is important that you handle this aspect of your family reunion with as much care and attention to detail as you do with the food events. You want to make sure everyone gets exactly what they ordered, particularly where sizes of clothing are concerned. You definitely don't want to run out of a specific size in the family reunion T-shirts and risk disappointing any family members. Therefore, if you offer commemorative materials it is important to keep a careful accounting of who ordered what, the quantities, sizes, and colors if applicable.

Depending on what commemorative items you offer, you can develop a simple record-keeping system. Start with a list of names of each person who will be receiving an item, the type of item, the size (if applicable), the quantity ordered, the unit price, the price extension, and an indication of whether payment has or has not been received.

It is always recommended that whoever is responsible for this function get a copy of each person's individual order. That way, if there are any questions, they can refer to the actual order. These can be placed in file folders in alphabetical order by surname for fast and efficient reference.

Special Events and Transportation - You may choose to conduct special events at your family reunion. These might include an outing to an amusement park, a trip to a battleground or national park, a tour, or a trek to some other location. You also may need to arrange for special transportation, such as passenger vans or charter buses to get there. In such cases, you want to identify the participants and collect money in advance to cover admission fees and transportation costs. A member of your team or a committee could then work on making advance arrangements and negotiating any fees or discounts.

A record-keeping system for special events and any transportation charges should also be a simple matter for you. Here is an example. Let's say your reunion will be held in Tampa, Florida over a long weekend and you plan to offer a trip to the Busch Gardens amusement park. Let's assume that interest is high and that forty members of your family want to go. It is probably cheaper to charter a bus for the entire group than to pay parking fees for ten to twelve cars. In this scenario, you would probably develop a per-person cost for adults and children that includes park admission and per-person bus fare. Food and other purchases would be handled individually at the park. You then would prepare a tracking list titled "Busch Gardens Outing" with columns labeled as follows:

Attendee name	Adult or child?	Price	Paid by:	Date paid	check #	boarded bus?
Alexander, John M.	Adult	$24.00	self	3/12/01	2101	
DeJournette, Florence	Adult	$24.00	self	3/14/01	3465	
Holder, Edward E.	Child	$12.00	mother	2/23/01	1020	
Holder, Green Berry	Child	$12.00	mother	2/23/01	5421	
Morgan, Samuel T.	Adult	$24.00	self	4/12/01	6565	
Morgan, William R.	Child	$12.00	father	3/8/01	654	

In this case, you have the name of every individual, the basis for the rate that they are being charged (adult or child), the unit price for that person, who paid (an essential consideration when dealing with family members who pay for others), and the date paid. You could even go so far as to add another column for check number. This record-keeping system will provide you with a roster to use when coordinating final counts with the amusement park and the transportation company. It also can be used as your attendee check-off list at the time of the event to make sure everyone is present and has boarded the bus.

Thank You Letters and Special Recognition - You will find as you work on your family reunion that you will have the opportunity to work with some wonderful people. These may be family members, friends, vendors, and business people of all types. When it comes time at the reunion to extend your thanks to the hardworking individuals, vendors, and businesses that made it a success, you don't want to omit anyone.

From the outset of the planning and organizing of your family reunion, it is a good idea to start a list of people to whom you intend to extend a thank you and/or special recognition. Your expression of appreciation may be as simple as a "stand up and be recognized" at the family banquet, or it may take the form of a special gift, a plaque, a specially customized T-shirt, or some other token. Your list can be as simple as a roster of names and the reason for which they are being thanked or recognized. After the reunion is over, you will also want to send a letter to each of the team members to thank them for their help. Whatever you do, don't omit this very important part of the reunion.

Summing Up

Record keeping, as you can see, is an important part of the reunion planning process. It can be as simple or complex as you make it. Many families working on their first reunion start small and keep their record keeping simple, confined to hand-written lists in spiral notebooks and on legal pads. For reunions held in subsequent years, they may decide to computerize some other functions. Others with family members conversant with computer programs such as spreadsheets, word processors, and databases may choose to mechanize some of the record-keeping functions the first year. Neither of these approaches is wrong. What *is* important is recognizing that record keeping is an essential part of planning and organizing your reunion. Good records keep you organized and focused. They also can prevent confusion among the team members and misunderstandings with other family members.

Invest the time up front to analyze your record-keeping needs and to set up record-keeping systems appropriate to each task area. You will save yourself a tremendous amount of time later trying to retrofit a morass of details into an orderly filing and record-keeping system.

Software Resources for Record Keeping

There are many software packages that can help you create a record-keeping system, including some that are specifically geared toward family reunions and genealogy.

Family Reunion Organizer - This Windows-based software package is published by FormalSoft, Inc., and provides the ability to create and maintain a family address book, schedules, budget and expense tracking reports, and task and assignment tracking reports. It can help you create mailing labels and nametags and a variety of other documents you might need for a reunion. It can even help you start creating a basic Web page. Visit their Web site at <http://www.family-reunion.com>.

Family Origins Version 8.0 Deluxe - *Family Origins* is a full-featured genealogy database software program published by FormalSoft, Inc., and Genealogy.com. One of its component functions concerns family reunions. It contains advice and location suggestions, and can produce helpful checklists. A free demo version of the program is available at the company's Web site at <http://www.familyorigins.com/demos.htm>.

Microsoft *Excel* - Microsoft Corporation's prestigious spreadsheet program can be used to produce budgets and to create family address lists and other data files. The nice things about using a spreadsheet program are that the basic functions are relatively simple to learn and that you can sort data in various fashions to produce reports. They are not great for producing mailing labels, nametags, and other utility documents.

Lotus 1-2-3 - Lotus Development Corporation's well-known *Lotus 1-2-3* spreadsheet program, like *Excel*, can be used to produce budgets and generate reports.

Microsoft *Access* - *Access* is a full-fledged database program that may be used to create and maintain databases of all types. There is a learning curve involved but you can structure highly effective databases and query them to produce reports, mailing lists, mailing labels, nametags, and just about anything else you want.

Questions to Ask Yourself

- What kinds of information do we need to compile and maintain?

- How should each set of record types be organized?

- Can each type of record be maintained manually or do we need computer software to help manage the data?

- Who will be responsible for keeping records for each type of information we need?

- What kind of reports will we need in order to monitor our progress and manage the reunion?

- If we need to use software, where will we acquire it? Who will install it? Who will input the data and produce reports?

- Are there record-keeping software and other resources on the Internet that can help us?

FoxPro - *FoxPro* is another sophisticated database program. Once an independent company, *FoxPro* is also owned by Microsoft. This database program also has the same capabilities as *Access*.

Quicken- One of the best personal accounting software programs is *Quicken*, published by Intuit, Inc. It can be used to manage income and expenses, write checks, categorize transactions, reconcile checking statements, and generate reports.

Internet Resources
Software for Record-Keeping Systems

There are a number of places on the Internet where you can locate software to help you with your reunion record keeping. Among the best are TuCows and CNET Networks, Inc.'s Download.com. Both sites provide access to software that you can download to your computer. Some of the software is freeware, and some are relatively inexpensive. At Download.com, you will also find free demo versions of many name-brand software packages that you can test before you buy the full-featured version. In order to locate appropriate software at these sites, use their search windows and enter keywords such as "reunion," "mailing," "mailing list," "database," "spreadsheet," etc.

Here are some examples of software from TuCows <http://www.tucows.com> at the time of this writing:

Mailing Lists
- Personal Mailing List - Mailing list database that can be sorted and which produces reports and mailing labels. $19.95
- Send It - Address book software that can be sorted, produce mailing labels and reports, and send e-mails (with attachments) to up to fifty addressees at once. $11
- Emailing List Pro - E-mail address book. $15

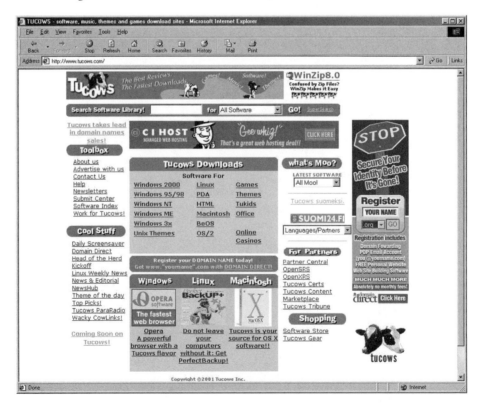

Here are some examples of software available from Download.com <http://down load.cnet.com> at the time of this writing:

Mailing Lists

- LabelPro 3.0 – Prints mailing labels on Avery products. FREE
- Mail Them – Mailing List management software. FREE

Family Reunion Software

- Reunion Planner – Address book, mailing labels, mail merge, photo and name badges, budget planner, and other functions. This is a demo version of the software; the full version is available for $59.95.

Visit software, electronics, and office supply stores to examine software packages and to compare prices. Often you can purchase software over the Internet less expensively, even including shipping charges, than you can buy in retail stores.

Brady Family Reunion, 1940

Chapter 5

Locating Family Members

While we will cover communications for your reunion in more detail in Chapter 6, it is important here to discuss whom you will invite, and how you will contact them. For your first family reunion, you may want to start small and choose to only invite members of your immediate or direct family line. You may then want to invite members of other branches of your family tree in subsequent years. On the other hand, you may decide to invite every relative you can locate to the first reunion, no matter how distant. It really is up to you.

No matter what you decide, you first have to locate family members in order to communicate with them and invite them to the reunion. The amount of effort you put into this will depend on a number of factors, including the size of your family, the type of reunion you are planning, how distantly related the family members are that you plan to invite, and where people are located. If some family members have been out of touch for many years or have moved a number of times, locating them may become something of a detective job.

In order to begin the communications process for the reunion with other family members, you will, at a minimum, want the following information:

- Contact name of the head of household for each family unit
- Complete mailing address (street address including apartment number if applicable, post office box, military address, and so on)
- ZIP code or other postal code
- Telephone number (including current area code) if possible

Any additional information that can be obtained, such as names of family members and e-mail addresses, is a bonus. However, it is not important at this juncture to have

---

In This Chapter ✔

- How to network with other family members to locate "lost" relatives

- How to use professional and other directories to locate people

- How to locate people's telephone numbers and e-mail addresses using Internet people search facilities

- Why you might want to hire a professional investigator

- Internet resources that can help

complete information about every member in a family group. That can be obtained later by mailing a Family Contact Form (see Appendix B) to each family unit and request that the family completes and returns it. It is sufficient to obtain the information listed above in some usable format regardless of whether it is handwritten, typed, or in a computerized format on a diskette. You can always rework or re-input it into whatever format you need later on.

There are many ways to locate family members. These include networking with family members you do know, checking directories of several types, using the many tools available on the Internet, and hiring a professional investigator. In this chapter, we will discuss each type of resource and some practical methods for using them successfully.

Networking with Your Relatives

The best starting point for locating family members is obviously through other family members. There is usually at least one person who keeps in touch with other members of the family on a regular basis. Often there is more than one person keeping the communication lines open. Thus there is at least one person in the family who has a detailed contact list or address book with which you can begin working.

In our family, I am the person sometimes referred to as "the great communicator." I am the keeper of the master telephone and address directory, and other family members often come to me when they need to contact one another. Once you locate the "communicator" in your family, ask if he or she would be willing to compile a master contact list for use in organizing the reunion. The person may respond that they know their list is incomplete, but you can encourage him or her to make contact and collaborate with other family "communicators" in order to compile as complete a list as possible. Offering to reimburse the person for his or her long distance telephone calls may help overcome some resistance.

Enlisting the help of one or more family members to compile the master family contact list has a number of benefits. First, you have someone already familiar with the family and its structure working to build the list, and that person will probably be able to easily spot gaps and track down the information to fill them. Second, you are involving one or more family members in the process and therefore getting their buy-in for the project. Third, in the course of the information gathering, word about the reunion will begin to spread and interest will grow. Finally, you will be able to delegate some work to other more qualified family members. You will find that using a network of family "communicators" is by far the most efficient and cost-effective method of building your initial communications contact list.

Using Professional and Other Types of Directories

Some missing relatives can be located using published directories. If you know where a missing relative went to school, contact the alumni association. It may be able to tell you if they have a current address for the person you are seeking, or it may be willing to sell you a copy of its current directory.

Directories published by professional organizations are another resource. Doctors, dentists, lawyers, and a wide variety of other people join professional organizations for the purpose of networking and sharing information. These organizations typically publish an annual member directory. An excellent resource for locating professional and trade organizations is the Internet Public Library Web site and its page titled "Associations on the Net" at <http://www.ipl. org/ref/AON>. Its collection of more than 2,000 Internet sites is searchable by keyword. For instance, I entered the keyword "dentist" and was presented with thirty matches. I entered the keyword "railroad" and was presented with seven matches, five of which represented railroad transportation professionals. The Web site can also provide information to assist you in contacting the respective groups. While not every person joins a professional organization, you may find invaluable leads to help you locate your missing relatives.

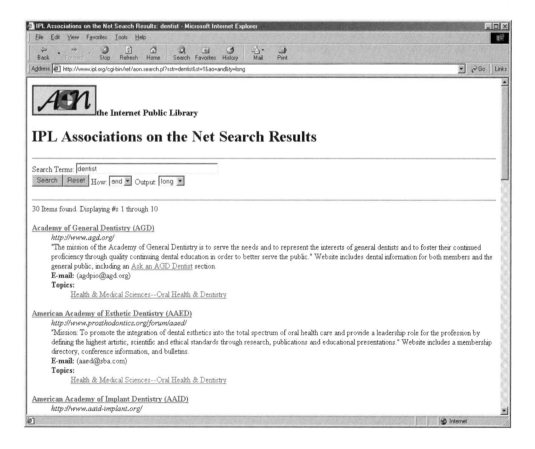

Internet Search Tools

With the advent of the Internet, our lives changed forever. All types of information are now available online, including a host of people search facilities to help locate people's names, addresses, telephone numbers, e-mail addresses and Web pages. These facilities allow us to type in one or more pieces of information that we know about an individual and to search for potential matches. The most common providers of people search facilities are telephone companies, network service providers, online directories, and online search engines. In almost all cases, the use of these facilities is free, paid for by the company and the advertisers that buy ad space on their Web site. One exception is USSEARCH.com, which offers two types of detailed searches for a fee. The less expensive one will probably suffice for locating your missing relative.

People search facilities provide an interim step you can use after your "communicators" have done their job and before you consider hiring a professional investigator. They can help you locate contact information for your "lost" family members. There are, however, a few caveats that need to be mentioned. First, the vast majority of information in these people search databases is culled from telephone number databases. If the missing family member has an unlisted telephone number, you probably will not find them using one of these facilities. Next, some of the people search databases are not cleaned up over time. New names and listings are merely added and little or no effort is made to remove inactive listings or make corrections. Be aware that some people search databases may have multiple e-mail addresses for the same person. Many people will change e-mail providers over time and people finder databases are almost never updated. Therefore, if you find more than one e-mail address for someone you believe is your relative, make note of all of them and be prepared to send an e-mail to each address in hopes that one of them is still current. Finally, be aware that none of these facilities is all-inclusive. You may need to conduct your search using several of them.

Here are some of the best of the people search facilities on the Internet:

SuperPages.com's People Pages - http://wp.superpages.com/people.phtml - SuperPages.com is a service of Verizon and allows you to search for people throughout the United States. It has built-in smart logic which presents alternate spellings of names. For example, I typed in the name Jeff Smith in South Carolina and was presented with matches for Geoffrey Smith, J. Smith, J. M. Smith, Jeffery Smith and Jeffrey Smith, all in addition to the name I typed. This is very helpful in the event you are unsure of the exact name used in the listing. In addition, you have the option of requesting that the search include nearby areas, a feature useful in the event your missing relatives lives in a suburb.

AnyWho - http://www.anywho.com - AnyWho is a service of AT&T which allows you to search for individuals and businesses. As one of the largest long distance carriers, it has a massive database of telephone listings and is one of the most reliable tele-

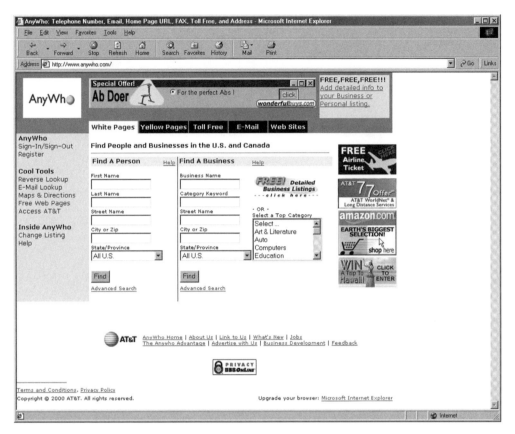

phone search facilities in terms of accuracy. Among what it calls its "Cool Tools" is a reverse look-up facility. If you have a telephone number and no name or address to go with it, go to the reverse look-up, type in the telephone number, and click on the Lookup button. If a match is found, you will be presented with the name and address associated with the listing. AnyWho is one of the facilities that is updated periodically; AT&T removes dead listings and adds new ones. You may also update your own listing by typing in changes online and then activating the changes by calling a toll-free number from your home telephone. The update is instantaneously available online.

Switchboard - http://www.switchboard.com - Switchboard.com is affiliated with CBS Broadcasting, Inc., and its data is provided by infoUSA.com. Switchboard is another service that allows you to locate telephone numbers and addresses for individuals and businesses. If you locate an individual in its database, you may then search for a match on an e-mail address.

Excite PeopleFinder - http://www.excite.com/peoplefinder - Excite is another online information directory and its PeopleFinder is powered by AT&T's AnyWho facility. Its database includes additional listings submitted and updated by Excite members. There is no e-mail search available in this tool.

Yahoo! People Search - http://people.yahoo.com - Yahoo! is the largest online information directory on the Internet. Its people search facility is powered by USSEARCH.com and allows you to enter a name and search for addresses and telephone numbers or to search for e-mail addresses.

WhoWhere - http://www.whowhere.lycos.com/wwphone/phone.html - WhoWhere is a service provided by Lycos, Inc., one of the other large online information directories. It provides telephone number, address, and e-mail address searches.

infoUSA.com (http://www.infousa.com/homesite/da.html) - Formerly known as Database America People Finder, infoUSA.com has been on the Internet for quite some time. Its Directory Assistance Web page provides a residential telephone number directory look-up facility, a business search, and a reverse telephone number search. It does not provide a search for e-mail addresses.

The Ultimates (http://www.theultimates.com) - The Ultimates is a compilation of several search facilities at one Web address. It provides access to white pages, yellow pages, and e-mail addresses, and contains an online trip planner. The white pages search uses six look-up facilities and also contains a reverse look-up feature. The Ultimates is a great metasearch tool for simultaneously searching multiple people search facilities.

In addition to the people search facilities discussed above, you can use Internet search engines to look for Web pages created by or containing the names of your missing relatives. With well over a billion Web pages on the Internet, you may be fortunate enough to find your relative. There are many good Internet search engines, among the best are:

- Google (http://www.google.com) – This simple, easy-to-use search engine boasts the largest index of Web pages on the Internet at the time of this writing.
- FastSearch (http://www.alltheweb.com) - This search engine is a creation of the Dell Computer Corporation and indexes the second largest number of Web pages, a very close second to Google.
- Alta Vista (http://www.altavista.com) – This search engine is a long-time player on the Web and also indexes a large percentage of Web pages.
- HotBot (http://www.hotbot.com) - The unique feature of this large search engine is its ability to take a name and search for all types of variations on it. For instance, if you input the name of actor James Stewart and select "the person" from the pull-down "Look for:" list, HotBot will search its index for James Stewart, Jim Stewart, and Jimmy Stewart. It will search for the names listed above separated with a middle name or initial. It also will search for the Stewart surname with first and/or middle initials.

Appendix A discusses the use of search engines and other Internet tools in great detail. You will want to read about techniques for effectively structuring your searches there. However, here are a few tips that can improve your rate of success when searching for people's names using a search engine:

- Type everything in lower case
- Enclose names in quotes
- Use Boolean searches
- Combine name and location

Hiring a Professional Investigator

Many families have missing relatives. They may have moved away, their addresses may have been lost or misplaced, or there may have only been communication between members of an older generation who are all now deceased. For whatever reason, the family may have lost touch with these individuals and you may want to reestablish communication and invite them to your family reunion.

A professional investigator may be able to locate some of your missing relatives for you but you may want to use this as a last resort. This is an expense for which you should budget if locating these people is important to a large number of your family members. Investigators' prices vary but are typically based on an hourly rate plus expenses.

You will need to provide an investigator with enough information to use as a beginning point to locate the missing person. This usually includes the full name, his or her birth date, a physical description or photograph, the last known address and time frame, the occupation, and any other information you might have. You can find listings of professional private investigators in the telephone yellow pages under "Investigators." You might also refer to the SuperPages.com Web site at <http://www.superpages.com>. Here you can search for investigators (and other businesses) by city and/or state. This can be especially useful if you are seeking people you know are in a particular area.

Combining Your Resources

You will probably find that using a combination of approaches to people finding resources is most successful. Always start with what you (and other family members) already know and compile the family contact list. Enlist the "communicators" to help you in this process. Follow that with the use of Internet-based people finder facilities to fill in the gaps. The use of search engines may provide some supplemental help for those missing relatives who have unlisted telephone numbers but who do have Web pages. If all else fails and you are unable to locate your missing relatives on your own, then consider using a professional investigator.

Locating lost or missing family members can be a time-consuming effort, but finding and welcoming them back into the fold can be exciting and rewarding. Reuniting family members who have not seen each other in a long time can be a cause of great celebration and will definitely make your family reunion a highly memorable event.

?

Questions to Ask Yourself

- Who is the "communicator" in your family?

- Are there other family members who maintain up-to date address books?

- Have we compiled a complete list of family members to invite to the reunion? If not, what resources do we need to use to locate "lost" family members:
  - —Professional and other directories
  - —Internet-based people search facilities
  - —Professional investigator

- Have we used a combination of resources to locate our family members?

- Are there Internet resources that can help us with our communications?

Internet Resources
To Help You Locate People

Professional Associations
- The Internet Public Library – http://www.ipl.org/ref/AON

Telephone Search Facilities
- Super Pages – http://wp.superpages.com/people.phtml
- AnyWho – http://www.anywho.com/
- Switchboard – http://www.switchboard.com/
- Excite PeopleFinder – http://www.excite.com/peoplefinder
- Yahoo! People Search – http://people.yahoo.com
- WhoWhere – http://www.whowhere.lycos.com/wwphone/phone.html
- InfoUSA.com – http://www.infousa.com/homesite/da.html
- The Ultimates – http://www.theultimates.com

Internet Search Engines

As mentioned before, Appendix A covers the use of search engines to locate Internet-based resources to assist in your reunion planning. Even if you are already using search engines, you will want to read Appendix A to learn where to obtain information about search engines and how to use them effectively. In the meantime, the following are among the best in terms of size and quality of information indexed.

- Google – http://www.google.com
- FastSearch – http://www.alltheweb.com
- Alta Vista – http://www.altavista.com
- HotBot – http://www.hotbot.com

Farnsworth Family Reunion, 1991

Chapter 6

Announcements and Ongoing Communications

From the very beginning, good communication is essential to hosting a successful family reunion. It is important that you get reunion information into the hands of all the family members you plan to invite as early as possible and to continue your communications to keep the interest level and excitement high. There are a variety of ways to do this, including using postal mail, e-mail, and creating a Web page for your family's reunion.

Depending on the type of reunion you plan to host and the number of people you plan to invite, the means and frequency by which you communicate will vary. A small, informal family reunion with a limited number of people obviously requires a less elaborate communication plan. You might be able to handle all your communications through telephone calls made by you

> **In This Chapter** ✔
>
> • Why good communications are essential to build a successful reunion
>
> • Different types of communication vehicles and documents
>
> • Using a reunion Web page
>
> • Using a MyFamily.com site
>
> • How to define a communication schedule for your reunion
>
> • Internet resources that can help

and/or a network of other family members. A reunion for a larger group of family members may require a more structured communication plan and schedule. Some families go to great lengths to communicate about and promote the family reunion while others adopt a more laid-back approach. For your first reunion, you probably want to expend more effort on communications because you are trying to generate a high level of interest the first time around. In subsequent years, however, you may not need to "sell" the reunion; a smaller number of mailings and word-of-mouth family network communications may be sufficient.

In this chapter, let's talk about a sample communications plan for larger reunions. We will talk about different types of documents, how to use them, and how to communicate with family members. We will also discuss how to create a communications schedule for the reunion. You may want to use this plan as your model, or you can customize your own communication plan by deleting documents suggested here or adding new ones. It really is up to you. You will find examples of the communication documents we discuss in Appendix B of this book. Remember that *your* family reunion is a unique event and that you will probably want to create announcements, invitations, and other communication documents that reflect your own family's individuality.

Communications for Large Reunions

Let's start with this scenario for your first family reunion. Suppose you have a large family consisting of a little over one hundred members, originally from St. Louis, Missouri. Of these one hundred members, there are twenty-five family units and you need to communicate with each of them. Fifteen family members still live in the vicinity but the remainder are scattered across the United States. It is mid-September and you are thinking of having the family reunion the first weekend in June of the following year. You therefore have approximately eight months in which to plan and organize the reunion. You know you will have to communicate a number of times with family members. How do you begin?

Compiling the Family Address Book

A family address book is an essential tool in your communications plan. Do you have the names, addresses, and telephone numbers of all the family units? If not, your first step is to do some legwork to compile a starter list. This usually involves making contact with other family members and requesting names, addresses, telephone numbers, and e-mail addresses. Start with someone who you know communicates frequently with other family members. The family historian or genealogist is generally one of your best information resources in this area. There may be someone else in the family who is the "great communicator" as we discussed in Chapter 5. Please recognize that some family members may have more current information than others, so it is always a good idea to ask when they last communicated with other family members.

Since you are going to be communicating a number of times with each family, it makes sense to take this information and create some sort of computerized mailing list database. You might want to use a word processor program such as Microsoft *Word* or *WordPerfect* and utilize its mail merge capabilities. Mail merge typically involves inputting names and addresses into one document and then using the program's facility for merging that data into another document for the purpose of creating mailing labels, customized letters, nametags, and other formatted documents.

If you obtain e-mail addresses for family members, you should consider setting up an e-mail distribution list to facilitate electronic communication with them. E-mail programs allow you to enter people's individual e-mail addresses, and most also allow you to build a distribution list of many people's e-mail addresses and assign it a name, such as "Family." Then, when you want to send an e-mail message to the entire group, simply type your message once and address it to "Family," and a copy of the message is sent to the e-mail addresses of everyone in your distribution list. This is a terrific time saver and, because e-mail is cheap, it is great for your budget, too!

If you are planning to produce a family address book for distribution to all family members, the residential mailing address and e-mail address, as well as telephone numbers, will ultimately be required.

The Series of Communications

There are a number of types of communications you will want to make to family units. In this large family reunion scenario, the following would be appropriate:

Family Reunion Survey - This document was discussed in Chapter 1. It is used to communicate the intent to host a family reunion. The survey solicits input to help determine the level of interest in the reunion and to identify the times of the year and

---

Family Reunion Survey

We are considering holding a family reunion for the descendants of John Paul Jones. In order to determine the interest level among the family and to begin developing a plan, we'd like to get your input concerning this event.

Please answer the questions below, and either mail it to Wally Jones at 123 Maple Lane, Family City, KS 55555 or send it to him via e-mail at wallyjones@address.com.

Your Name: _____

Your Address: _____

_____

Telephone: (____) _____-_____ E-mail: _____@_____

Number of persons in your family: _____

Are you interested in attending a family reunion? YES   NO

What time of year is best for your family to attend? (Please indicate best month)
JAN FEB MAR APR MAY JUNE JULY AUG SEPT OCT NOV DEC

Is there another time you would consider as a second choice? (Please indicate best alternative month)
JAN FEB MAR APR MAY JUNE JULY AUG SEPT OCT NOV DEC

How many persons would be able to attend the reunion?
Adults: _____ Children ages 0-6: _____ Children ages 7-12: _____
Children ages 13-16: _____ Seniors: _____

We are considering having the reunion in Family City, Kansas, because there are so many family members located in that area. Would you attend the reunion if it were held there?   YES   NO

Are there any other areas you would consider as a site for the family reunion?
YES   NO   If so, where? _____

Would you and/or one of your family members be willing to participate on the planning committee for the reunion? YES NO   If so, who can participate?
_____

If you cannot help on the planning committee, would you and/or one of your family members be willing to help on-site at the reunion? YES NO
If so, who can participate?
_____

Our reunion will include meals and some commemorative memento of the occasion. There will therefore be a per person cost to attend the reunion that we will communicate to you at a later date. There will be a price for adults and a lower price for children and seniors.

Thank you for your input to the process! We'll communicate the results back to you soon.

Wally Jones

---

locations that would be convenient for the family to attend. (See the Family Reunion Survey in Appendix B of this book.) The inclusion of a self-addressed, stamped envelope (SASE) always encourages the recipient to respond.

Family Contact Form - Up-to-date contact information is essential for your successful communication with family members. The sample form included in Appendix B of this book can be used or adapted for your family's use. The form can be mailed with the Family Reunion Survey, with the reunion registration package, or by itself. Don't forget to include a SASE.

Let's say that the survey results are in and, based on the responses, the consensus is that the reunion should be held in the family's hometown of St. Louis. You may not have made arrangements for the precise location yet, but it is important to begin getting the word out to family members that there will, indeed, be a family reunion.

Reunion Announcement - It is time to begin generating interest and excitement in the family reunion. Start by designing an announcement that contains the essential, pertinent information about the reunion. Your announcement can take the form of a one-page flyer or a postcard. (A postcard is cheaper to mail but may lack the visual impact of a larger document.) In the scenario we are developing here, the important points to be communicated in the flyer are:

- There will be a family reunion
- It will be in St. Louis
- It will be a wonderful, fun event
- Look for details in a future mailing
- Contact name, number, and call for volunteers to help

A copy of a sample announcement can also be found in Appendix B of this book.

In Chapter 2, we discussed organizing for success. It was there that we talked about recruiting family members to work with you and forming committees to develop the details of the reunion. This involves working with the entities described in Chapter 3 such as hotels to select a location, family members and/or caterers to arrange for meal functions, vendors for commemorative clothing and other items, hired personnel, transportation companies, and others. As the details are finalized, you will be working on the budget and the per-person cost for the reunion, optional events, and commemorative items. When you have all this information in hand, it will be time for the next and most important communication document—the registration package.

The Registration Package - The single most important communication to family members will be the registration package. It should have strong visual impact and

Meet Me in St. Louis!

The MORGAN Family Reunion 2001

~~~~~~

**We're very happy to announce the third annual
MORGAN family reunion,
to be held this year in St. Louis, Missouri!**

We surveyed the family and the results are in! The consensus is that we will meet in St. Louis for three days of family fun from July 28-30, 2001. We've negotiated an excellent, discounted rate with a local hotel and have obtained discounted tickets to a Cardinals baseball game for everyone! While we're there, we'll also have a wonderful family banquet at the hotel.

Watch your mail for the registration packet which we'll be mailing within the next month. It will contain your registration form as well as details about the reunion, brochures about the attractions in St. Louis, reservation instructions for the hotel, maps of the area, and information about local transportation. In addition, there will be ordering information for our annual commemorative reunion T-shirts.

**This year's reunion promises to be the best ever,
and you *don't* want to miss it!**

Mark your calendars NOW!

For questions, please contact Cousin Ed at (212) 555-5555.

should be intended to generate excitement in the event. The package is best mailed in a large envelope. You don't want to send the registration information via e-mail, even though you may have e-mail addresses for many of your relatives. An e-mail message lacks visual excitement and is likely to be sent to just one person in the family. The chance that it may be lost, deleted, or otherwise not seen by all family members is great. The contents of the reunion registration package should provide all the detailed information necessary for the family to make its decision about attending the event. It should be thorough in its descriptions of all items and should be meticulously correct. Therefore, it is a good idea to have several people on your team review it for accuracy and clarity before you mail the package. The types of information you will want to include in the registration package are as follows:

- Begin with a cover letter filled with exciting details. It should announce the reunion again, this time with all the details. It should include the name of the family reunion, a logo or some graphic (especially if a special one has been prepared for the reunion), the date, the location, descriptions of the events, a brief agenda (if it has been prepared by that time), and information about any commemorative clothing or other items that may be offered for order in advance or for sale at the reunion. If there are any cut-off dates for registration or for ordering commemorative items, make sure you include them and highlight them in boldface type. The cover letter should also include the name, telephone number, and e-mail address of one or more people who may be contacted to answer questions. (Please see the example of the Registration Package Cover Letter in Appendix B.)

- A registration form should be included with spaces to list the names and ages of every family member who will attend the reunion. The form should clearly list the per-person costs for the reunion itself for all age categories, the cost for any optional events and transportation, ordering information for any commemorative items (including color and size if appropriate), menu choices for any meal event, if applicable, and a space to indicate any special needs for any attendee. These might include special dietary restrictions, handicapped access, and seating preferences in the event you offer smoking and non-smoking sections at a banquet or other event. Again, if there are any cut-off dates for registrations for the reunion, the hotel, meals, optional events, or for ordering commemorative items, make sure you include statements to that effect on the registration form and highlight it in boldface type. (Please see the sample Registration Form in Appendix B.)

- Check your records to determine if you have received a Family Contact Form. If not, you will want to include one in the mailing.

- The hotel you select may have brochures about its facilities and you may want to include one of these in the mailing. This will provide family members with detailed information about hotel accommodations and telephone numbers for reservations.

- If you are planning any optional excursions and are able to obtain brochures or promotional literature, you may want to include these in the package.

> Always include a self-addressed stamped envelope (SASE) with your registration package mailing. You want to encourage the completion and return of the registration form and to make it as simple as possible.
>
> **For Your Information**

- A map of the area and other brochures, such as those from the local chamber of commerce, might be included in your package.
- Always include a self-addressed stamped envelope (SASE). You want to encourage the completion and return of the registration form and to make it as simple as possible.

In Chapter 4, we discussed record-keeping systems and the importance of tracking the family members' response to every mailing. You therefore will want to record to whom you mailed the registration package, and record each response you receive. At some point, you will want to follow up with those family members who have not responded. Your first follow-up can take the form of a letter, such as the sample included in Appendix B. A second and final follow-up may be done by telephone. You don't want to annoy people, but you want to get some response one way or another. A telephone call is a type of personal communication that makes the family member feel wanted and encourages him or her to respond.

In some cases, you will find that the registration package has been lost or misplaced, and you will want to send a replacement package as soon as possible. In your mailing record-keeping system, record the date of any follow-up and/or the mailing of another registration package. If you still don't get a response, be prepared to make another follow-up telephone call.

You will find that some family members may want a confirmation of their registration. It is a good idea to include a sentence in your registration package, both in the letter and on the registration form, that states "Your cancelled check is your receipt and confirmation of your reservation for the reunion." Make sure people understand that they should make their own travel and hotel reservations.

Many family members may send in their registrations months in advance of the event. Others may wait until the last minute. It is important to keep your reunion foremost in the minds of all the family members. Therefore, another mailing forty-five to sixty days in advance of the event can help keep interest and anticipation at a high level.

The Hype Mailing - This next mailing is intended to remind those family members who have registered for the reunion to recheck their calendars and mark the event. It can also be used to remind those who haven't yet registered to get on the ball. Some family members may have procrastinated (Yes, we all have procrastinators in the family tree!) and need a little shove. The hype mailing may be as simple as an oversized postcard or it can be another letter or flyer sent in an envelope. You can also supplement and reinforce a postal mailing by sending an e-mail to everyone on your family e-mail distribution list. The types of information you want to include in the hype mailing are:

- The name of the family reunion, along with any special graphic or logo developed for the occasion

- The date
- The location
- The fact that the event is getting closer
- "Be there or be square!"
- For more information, or if you haven't yet registered, contact...

Throughout the process, from mailing the survey until the date of the reunion, you will want to maintain communication with all the family members. That means setting up a record-keeping system such as the one we discussed in the last chapter and tracking each mailing and following up is necessary. Unless a family member specifically asks to be removed from the mailing list, continue to mail materials to him or her throughout the process. You never know whether someone is procrastinating, but you want each family member to feel that it's never too late to decide to attend. Always be prepared to accept registrations up to the last minute, and to accommodate and welcome any family members who are unexpected walk-in arrivals on the day of the reunion. (You may have to make arrangements with the caterer for additional meals but you certainly want everyone to feel welcome to attend.)

A Reunion Web Page

Another effective means of communicating information about your family reunion is to set up a Web page. There are many places on the Internet that provide free space for people's Web pages. GeoCities, a subsidiary of Yahoo!, for example, is a major provider of free Web space for individuals. Check its Web site at <http://geocities.yahoo.com/home>. RootsWeb, one of the major genealogical Web sites, also provides unlimited Web page space. Information about space on its servers can be found at <http://accounts.rootsweb.com>.

A family reunion Web page can be a very effective communication vehicle for people who have access to the Internet. Creating a Web page at GeoCities, for instance, is a simple and intuitive exercise in which you select from a set of templates and simply enter text. You can also add graphics and photographs easily. Your Web page can contain the announcement information, details about the reunion venue, a copy of the registration form, and anything else you would

like to include. It is important to keep the Web site updated with current information and to use it to help generate excitement. Perhaps one of the teenagers familiar with Web page design would be willing to assume the role of family webmaster. After the reunion, the Web page can be a place to post photographs and may even become a year-round family communication vehicle.

If you decide to create a Web page, you can then include the Web address on every piece of printed material you mail and as part of the signature block of your e-mail to all the family members on your distribution list.

The MyFamily.com Site

MyFamily.com, Inc. is a leader in the area of family history research. It, along with its sister sites, Ancestry.com, FamilyHistory.com and RootsWeb.com, provides the broadest, most comprehensive Internet-based materials about genealogy. The MyFamily.com Web site can provide you, the family reunion planner and organizer, with a tremendous communication facility for your entire family. It provides at no charge a private online environment in which you can build a custom, Internet-based site for your family to share information. You can publish text, post photographs, and create a family address book of names, addresses, telephone numbers, and e-mail addresses. You can set up a calendar of birthdays, anniversaries, and other events, and send e-mail reminders to people. You can get together for online chats in a private family chat room and, with the use of free downloadable software, you can even hold voice conversations with other people in your chat room. And, you don't need any experience building Web sites to create a fully functioning family site.

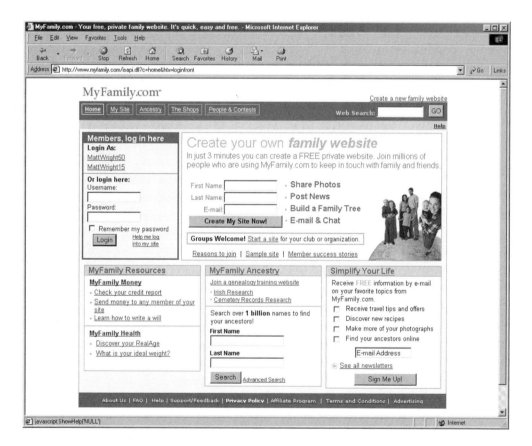

Not only does the MyFamily.com facility provide an excellent tool for promoting your family reunion, it is the perfect vehicle for on-going family communication. You will want to visit the MyFamily.com Web site at <http://www.myfamily.com> to see all that it has to offer.

Defining a Communication Schedule for Your Reunion

By now you should have a good understanding of the types of communication facilities available to you. These include documents and Internet-based materials for use in communicating with family members and promoting the family reunion to them. One of the things you must consider, however, is the schedule of communications. Hopefully you have decided to host a family reunion with enough lead time to communicate with family members and allow them the opportunity to respond at their own pace.

In previous chapters we discussed many of the forms of communication between you and other family members. Now it's time to put it all together in a practical example. Let's use the scenario we developed earlier in the chapter and define a sample communications schedule for a family reunion. Assume that we will begin our brainstorming in early September for a reunion to be held in June of the following year. Keep in mind that for any mailing you do, family members will need time to review the material you mailed and make a decision. Often family members will need to consult their calendars and make arrangements with employers and others before they can respond. You therefore want to build a communication schedule that allows for a reasonable response time. Let's talk about each of the communications we discussed earlier, but this time we will focus on timing, scheduling, and follow-up dates.

Compiling the Family Address Book - Once you begin in earnest to compile the family address book, it may take you a couple of weeks to get the information together and to prepare mailing labels.

Family Reunion Survey - The survey can be prepared at the same time the family address book is being compiled. That means typing, editing, and photocopying it, as well as preparing SASEs for inclusion in the mailing. Once the survey is mailed, a response time of between two and three weeks is reasonable.

At the end of three weeks, you might want to send a follow-up letter to the family members to whom you mailed the survey who have not responded. (If you have a smaller group, you might find making a telephone follow-up call is preferable.) In the meantime, you can always contact the people who have responded and clarify any responses you don't understand.

If you still have not received some responses at the end of another week to ten days, you may want to make one more follow-up call. Don't be a pest, but see what you can elicit in a telephone conversation. Let's face it, some people just don't like to fill out surveys.

Reunion Announcement - After the surveys have been returned and you have had the opportunity to tabulate and evaluate the responses, you should have a good idea of the interest level for a family reunion. Proceeding on the assumption that the reunion will take place, you now need to form your planning and organization team and begin making arrangements. At the same time, you need to officially announce the reunion and start generating some excitement. A good-looking, oversized postcard with some exciting text and graphics announcing the reunion can be prepared and photocopied or printed. Apply a mailing label and postage and start getting the word out. You may want to add a contact name and telephone number and a call for volunteers to help participate.

Reunion Registration Package - As you proceed with the process, you should decide on the contents of the reunion registration package. If you want brochures from hotels, chambers of commerce, and other places, ask your team members to request such materials from the vendor representatives with whom they are working.

Once you have the actual details of date and location worked out, your budget prepared, and your registration fees determined, it's now time to start preparing the reunion registration package. Prepare the cover letter, a registration form, the mailing labels, and the SASEs, and gather together any other materials you plan to include in the package. Double and triple check everything in it for accuracy. Make the mailing and keep a record of the family members to whom the packages are mailed.

Allow forty-five to sixty days for people to respond with their registrations. Use your mailing tracking system to keep track of who has responded and paid their registrations. You will want to telephone those who have not responded and encourage them to do so. If you have a large number of families who have not responded, you might need to divide this responsibility among several team members or volunteers. Remember, the focus during your follow-up is to promote a positive experience and generate excitement about how much fun everyone will have at the reunion. Some people may tell you right away that they cannot or will not attend the reunion, and you should make a notation in your records so no one calls to follow up with them again. People who tell you they are still trying to decide can be followed up with later as necessary. Be prepared to respond to requests for the mailing of replacement registration packages as some may be lost, misplaced, or never received.

Thirty days after the first follow-up, if there are family members who still have not responded with a registration, make another telephone call or send a letter or an e-mail. Let them know they will be missed if they can't attend the reunion. Ask if there are any questions or concerns, and offer to answer any questions they may have. At this point, this is about all you can do. You don't want to risk angering or alienating anyone. A second follow-up telephone call should probably be all that you make. If you don't have a response, drop it.

The Hype Mailing – This mailing should be done no more than thirty days in advance of the family reunion. Your goal is to reinforce the interest and excitement of those families who have already registered and to generate last-minute interest by those who have not yet registered.

Based on the timetable we discussed above, the following is a schedule for the mailings and follow-ups for a June family reunion:

DATE	MAILING or ACTIVITY
September 15	Compile Family Address Book information
October 1	Mail Family Reunion Survey
October 22	First follow-up on Family Reunion Survey
November 1	Second follow-up on Family Reunion Survey
November 15	Mail the Reunion Announcement
January 1	Mail Reunion Registration Package
March 1	First follow-up on registrations
April 15	Second follow-up on registrations
May 1	Send the Hype Mailing
May 15	Third and final follow-up on registrations
June 1	FAMILY REUNION TIME!

The schedule has ample time built in to allow for a comfortable succession of mailings and follow-ups. It could be somewhat compressed, but you still want to allow ample time for family members to review the materials that you mail and make their decision as to whether to attend or not. It is important not to pressure family members for fear of alienating them. You want them to be excited by the prospect of a family reunion and to happily anticipate it at each stage of the planning and announcement process.

You may find that there is a need for additional mailings other than the ones described above. For example, you may be planning a children's event such as the "I'm My Own Grandpa" party described in Chapter 8. That party involves a dress-up component and it may be appropriate to design another mailing or e-mail to the children's parents to describe the event and suggest materials to be used for costumes. You will need to decide where in chronological sequence that and other communications need to be made. In this example, a communication of some sort should be sent to family members who have children and who have already received and returned their paid registrations. However, it should also be sent far enough in advance for parents to make preparations for their children to participate, i.e., to locate costume materials.

Designing attractive and informative letters, announcements, registration forms, and other documents can be a great deal of fun. People enjoy using their imagination to create vibrant, artistic, and exciting materials like these. You are certain to have people on your team who will leap at the chance to work on the family communications as long as they have the opportunity to use their creativity.

Your commitment to good communications throughout the reunion planning process cannot be stressed enough. Doing a good job will provide a momentum to the project that keeps the excitement and anticipation among family members running high. Postal mail and e-mail can really be combined to facilitate your communications to family members. The use of a frequently updated Web page or an exciting Internet-based family site such as MyFamily.com can not only facilitate communications, but can become an often referred-to electronic bulletin board for ongoing updates on the progress of the reunion. The possibilities are endless! All you have to do is determine what communications you need and want to make to family members, define the schedule, create the materials, and send them out. Your excellent communications will go a long way in guaranteeing the success of your family reunion.

Questions to Ask Yourself

- What are the different types of communications vehicles we plan to use to promote attendance at our reunion?

- What are the component pieces of each one of these communications vehicles?

- Have we developed a communication schedule?

- Could we set up a Web page for our family reunion and use that as a communication tool? If so, who can create and maintain it?

- Have we considered creating a MyFamily.com site and using it to foster family communications and promote our reunion?

- Are there Internet resources that can help us with our communications?

Internet Resources
To Help With Communications

Places to Build and Host Web Pages
- MyFamily.com – http://www.myfamily.com
- RootsWeb – http://accounts.rootsweb.com
- GeoCities – http://geocities.yahoo.com/home

Internet Resources for Invitations and Other Materials

- Reunion Station - A source for printed invitations for your family reunion. http://www.reunionstation.com/

- Better Homes and Gardens – Tips Concerning Invitations – Information about, and samples of, different family reunion invitations. http://www.bhglive.com/food/cookhelpers/reunion/reunion9.html

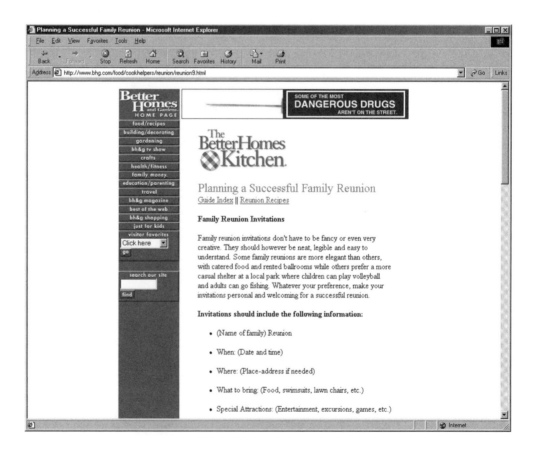

- Better Homes and Gardens - Printable Family Reunion Invitations - Invitations you can print from the Web and photocopy onto your own invitation card stock.
  http://www.bhglive.com/food/cookhelpers/reunion/reunion10.html

- Registration Form by FormalSoft, Inc. - A simple registration form sample you might use to create your own registration form.
  http://family-reunion.com/register.htm

- Hall of Names International, Inc.'s Family Reunion Registration Form - Web page containing a variety of reunion-related registration information, including a sample registration form.
  http://www.myroots.com/reunion.htm#Registration

In Appendix A, I discuss the use of search engines and other Internet tools in detail. Many families have created registration forms for their own reunions and placed them on the Web. Go to your favorite search engine(s) and enter:

"family reunion" registration

You will be rewarded with links to many samples of online registration forms. You might consider adapting one of these formats to your own printed or Web-based registration form.

- ERSVP - A professional event planning and reservation company that can handle invitations and reservations, as well as collect and manage finances for a large reunion of other event.
  http://www.eRSVP.com

Holder Family Reunion, ca. 1900

Chapter 7

On-Site Preparations and Set-Up

Throughout the planning and registration process, you and your team members have been working with people concerning the hotel or other venue, catering, entertainment, and other services. You have been compiling information about attendance for your reunion and tracking registrations. Commemorative items have been ordered and received. Hopefully all of the arrangements have been made by now. However, just because the contracts are signed and registrations are in, that doesn't mean you should relax just yet.

It is important to create a checklist to ensure that everything is ready to go. The team members responsible for various areas should also be ready to provide names of people who can and will be available to help on-site. Most importantly, you want to schedule meetings and walkthroughs to review everything related to facilities, catering and food, entertainment, transportation, and any other services for which you have contracted. Here are some suggestions for how to proceed with these reviews:

In This Chapter

- How checklists aid in the on-site operations of your reunion

- Why you should communicate with all vendors providing services just before the reunion begins

- Enlisting help from other family members to act as hosts or coordinators

- Organizing the distribution of your attendee packages, and commemorative T-shirts or other items

Hotel - If your reunion involves the use of any hotel facilities, you should schedule a meeting with a member of the marketing staff of the hotel. This meeting can take place at least one or more days prior to the reunion. That way, any problems with the facilities can be resolved before family members begin to arrive. By now, you should have a good idea of the final count of attendees. Based on these numbers and the activities you have planned, you and the hotel can confirm such things as meeting room and banquet set-ups. This is also the time to reconfirm details concerning things like placement of signage, the availability and set-up of registration and information tables, your ability to put up welcome banners and decorations, the serving of alcoholic beverages (and any bar/bartender arrangements), availability of handicapped accommodations, procedures concerning emergencies, the validation of parking tickets, and other details. If the cost of your use of meeting rooms is to be covered as a result of the total number of sleeping rooms used by members of your family, this is also the time to confirm and finalize those arrangements. Make certain you and a member of the hotel's marketing office physically walk through every meeting room and other facility you are scheduled to use. Be on the lookout for existing damage to the facility, such as torn wallpaper, chipped paint, and broken lighting fixtures. Make sure it is understood that these problems existed before your group uses the facility. You do not want the hotel to charge you for pre-existing damage.

Park Site - If you plan to use a park as the site of your reunion, it is a good idea to make contact with the park ranger or administrator at least a week in advance. Introduce yourself and let him or her know about your reunion and how many persons you expect to attend. Ask about the space you will be using and make sure it is reserved. It is not altogether rare for a family to show up at a site it has reserved for a family gathering only to find another group there and no one available with the authority to resolve the situation. Inquire about the condition of the park and its facilities and about any additional permits required or special usage rules you should know.

Catering and Food - Some family members, to a large degree, will measure your reunion's success by the quantity and quality of the food presented. During the planning process of your reunion, you will have identified the events at which food is to be served. Depending on the type of reunion and the types of food you select, your checklist in this area will vary. In the case of a family picnic or barbecue, your list may be relatively simple, consisting of names of family members and the food they plan to bring. If you have planned a more structured reunion and have arranged for the catering of one or more meals, your checklist may be more involved. Some families arrange for a per-person price for buffet dining in a hotel restaurant, and this works especially well for breakfasts where the hotel already has a breakfast bar. Not everyone will get up in time to have breakfast, so you are not paying for food that is not being eaten. You may also arrange for dinner, and tell family members that they are on their own for breakfast and lunch. If you are hosting a formal banquet, schedule a meeting with the caterer or food service providing the meal. You might also want to include the hotel marketing representative in this meeting to ensure that everyone has the same expectations about the event and so that the logistical details can be settled in one meeting. Review the menu with the caterer again and reconfirm all of the food arrangements. This is the time to provide the caterer with the final counts of adults, children, and seniors to be served, and any special dietary requirements for any family members. Providing the caterer with advance notice of any special meals helps ensure that everyone is served promptly and that there is no confusion or misunderstanding at the time of the banquet. Verify with the caterer that you may see and sample the food just in advance of the banquet. At that time, you can reconfirm that special dietary dishes have, in fact, been prepared and are ready to be served.

Entertainment - If you have arranged for entertainment at your reunion, you will want to schedule a meeting on-site just prior to the event. Most entertainers like to see the venue in advance. This allows them to check their working space, electrical connections, acoustics, and other logistics. This allows you the opportunity to communicate the size and character of the audience and provide details about how and when the entertainment is to be delivered.

Florists - If you have engaged a professional florist to create centerpieces and other arrangements for your reunion, make a telephone call to him or her at least a week in advance. Reconfirm the date, time, and location to which the floral arrangements are to be delivered for your reunion. If you have had a larger number of registrations than you first expected, your banquet may be larger and require more tables. In that case, you may also require more centerpieces, and now is the time to change your order with the florist. You want to give him or her ample time to order and receive all the components for the arrangements so that each one is alike. At this point, ask the florist to verify the number of pieces and the pricing.

Photographers and Videographers - Professional photographers and videographers seldom need much instruction. However, you should make contact with any you have engaged several days before the reunion. Reconfirm the date, location, and time of the event and discuss the service they will provide. Let them know how many people you expect them to photograph and what types of photographs are required, such as candid shots, family portraits, and large group shots. This allows them to come prepared with the right camera equipment, film, lighting, and other ancillary equipment. Ask the photographer and/or videographer to meet you on-site thirty minutes before the event so you can describe what will take place at the event and give them any last minute instructions.

> Let the photographer know how many people you expect them to photograph and what types of photographs are required, such as candid shots, family portraits, and large group shops. This allows them to come prepared with the right camera equipment.
>
> **For Your Information** ⓘ

Transportation Carriers - If your reunion includes any side trips for which you arranged commercial transportation, you will want to meet with a representative of the company just prior to the reunion. The carrier will need to know the final count of passengers in order to provide the correct size and number of vehicles. Reconfirm the date, time and location of departure, the destination, and the date, time, and location for the return trip. If there are family members with disabilities participating in the trip, make sure the carrier is aware so that handicap accommodations are available on the vehicles provided. Provide the carrier with a contact name and phone number of someone at the reunion site who will act as the coordinator for the trip. This person should also accompany the group as host and identify him- or herself to the driver(s) before the time of departure.

When you negotiated a contract with each of the service providers, there was probably a clause concerning the method and timing of payment. The hotel, caterer, and florist probably require payment in advance. The transportation carrier probably requires payment at the time of departure. The entertainers, photographer, and videographer may require payment at the time of the reunion or immediately thereafter. Be sure to check each contract so that you understand when payment is due, and make arrangements with your treasurer to have checks or other required forms of payment ready at the appropriate time.

What has been described so far concerns working with vendors and other professionals, but there are many aspects of the reunion that will be handled by family members. Prior to the event, you want to prepare a checklist for these items and activities to ensure that everything is in order. Here are examples of the areas you want to check:

Welcome Area/Registration Desk - A welcome area or a registration desk/table is an important component for most family reunions. At a smaller event, this is where everyone signs the guest book, updates their contact information, gets their nametags, and learns about the activities scheduled for the reunion. For a larger reunion, this may be the location for sign-in, nametags, distribution of attendee packages, verification of payments, pick-up of commemorative clothing and other items, sign-up for side trips, and general information. It can also be the central greeting center and information desk for the duration of the reunion, if you like. You will need to make a checklist of materials to be stocked and maintained there, and you will need to establish a schedule for people to work the desk.

Attendee Packages - Decide in advance what items will go into an attendee package. Nametags, a reunion schedule, a newsletter, a list of registered attendees, a map of the area, brochures about local attractions and events, tickets for drawings or raffles, information about side trips and transportation, and other items are all appropriate.

Nametags - Nametags are a critical component of your reunion. Decide in advance whether you want people to make their own nametags or if you want to produce them with a computer. Whatever you decide, make sure people have at least one nametag for each day of the event. Make sure you have extras available at your information desk.

Commemorative Items - Confirm that the items have been ordered *and received*. If the shipment has not been received, someone needs to take responsibility to follow up and track its progress. If it has been received, boxes need to be opened immediately and inspected for damage, and adjustments need to be made. If you ordered items that come in sizes, such as T-shirts, someone should sort them by size and count them. Group items by size and label the cartons. It is far easier and more efficient to distribute sized items when presorting has already been done.

Signage - Signs should be prepared in advance and packaged to be taken to the reunion site. Notes can be made on the back of the sign to indicate where it is to be placed or used.

Decorations - If you plan to place your own decorations, make a list of all the supply items required. Don't forget tape, scissors, pushpins or thumbtacks, and a small tool kit.

First-Aid Kit - Make sure you are prepared for small emergencies by having a first-aid kit on hand. The kit should be kept in a central, easily accessible location and everyone should be made aware of its existence and location. (You might include a note in the attendee package about the kit and the telephone numbers for local emergency units.)

Hosts and Coordinators - It is a good idea to have family members act as hosts or coordinators for every event during your reunion. Someone may coordinate the softball game, another may host the children's party, and someone else can accompany a group on a side trip and coordinate the details for the trip.

Every family reunion is different, and your checklist will need to reflect the unique character and activities of *your* reunion. It takes a little thoughtful evaluation of your reunion schedule of events and attendees to devise a checklist. Once you have your list, review it for completeness. Then arrange the activities and follow-ups in a chronological sequence and assign scheduled dates for each item. Voila! You now have your complete checklist. By following through on each action item, you can easily maintain control and not miss a single important detail. Your follow-through at this stage is another key to guaranteeing the success of your family reunion.

Questions to Ask Yourself

- Have we thought through our entire reunion agenda and prepared checklists for each activity?

- Who will take responsibility for each of these areas?

- Have we scheduled on-site meetings with our caterer, vendors, and entertainers just before the reunion so they can see the facility, understand what is expected of them, and get any last minute information?

- Have we met with hotel staff, park staff, or other administrators to brief them about our reunion and provide them with a schedule?

- Have we determined all the component items for the attendee packages?

- Who will staff the welcome area/registration desk to greet attendees and distribute materials? Will the schedule allow volunteers to attend activities?

Cousins reunited at the Weatherly Family Reunion, 2000

Chapter 8

Ice Breakers, Mixers, and Games

Family reunions are occasions for the renewal of relationships between family members, the introduction of new family members, and the building of new bonds between family members of all ages. Enjoyable conversation, interaction, and shared experiences are key ingredients for the success of the gathering. In many cases, bringing people together is enough to get things started. However, sometimes you have to help things along, and in this chapter we will discuss some ways to promote communication and interaction between family members that will help make your reunion more successful.

> **In This Chapter** ✔
>
> - Why nametags are essential and how to produce them
> - Games and other activities that promote communication and interaction
> - Ways to make sure all age groups are involved
> - Outdoor games
> - Internet resources that can help

Nametags

One of the most basic and effective tools you can use at your family reunion is nametags. Some family members will, of course, recognize one another immediately, but bear in mind that some people may not have seen one another in years. Also, children grow quickly and physically change as they mature. Nothing can promote recognition and spur conversation more quickly than the use of nametags. They provide a way for people to quickly and easily identify one another, and at the same time remove any anxiety about having to remember everybody's name. The information on the nametag can vary depending on what you want it to accomplish. If it is strictly to communicate a person's name, then that's all that should be written on the nametag. If you want to use the nametag as a tool for some other activity, such as a group mixer or a game, more information may be needed.

There are several ways to approach the making of nametags. One way is to have family members make nametags for themselves as they arrive at the reunion. Set up a table with a couple of chairs, a good supply of blank nametags, markers and crayons, and perhaps a large cardboard sample of the information that should be written on the nametag. You might consider separate sign-in/nametag tables for adults and children, and let the children be creative with coloring their own nametags with crayons and markers. (Adults may want to do this too!)

Another way to produce nametags is with a computer. You can use most word processing programs, such as Microsoft *Word* or *WordPerfect*, to produce nametags. The programs usually come with templates that can be used with standard Avery label nametags, both the self-adhesive variety and the cardboard type that inserts into a plastic holder that can be pinned or clipped onto clothing. If, as we discussed in an earlier chapter, you decided to use a database program and build your registration database, your family computer expert may be able to extract all the information you want for your nametags and produce them for you.

If you are hosting a multi-day reunion, it is always a good idea to have multiple nametags available for each person. The self-adhesive variety really is not reusable, so be sure to have a fresh supply of nametags available for each day. Always have extra, blank nametags available for walk-ins, people who lose them, and people who change clothing during the day. Whatever you do, don't forget to make nametags for babies.

Information you might want to include on a nametag:

- First name
- Middle name or initial
- Surname
- Family line of descent (names of parents or grandparents)
- Maiden name
- City and state of residence
- Age (sometimes a sensitive issue)

Does this is seem like a lot of information for a nametag? Perhaps, but it also can be a source of data for an icebreaker, mixer, or a family game.

Mixers and Games

Hundreds of books have been written that include hundreds of different games that help to get members of a group interacting with each other. Some examples are:

Family Information Scavenger Hunt - A great way to get people talking and exchanging information about one another is to organize a family information scavenger hunt. In advance of the reunion, prepare a simple list with ten to twenty questions concerning information you already know about family members who will be attending the reunion. Here are some sample questions:

- Which family or family member came the longest distance to the reunion?
- Who is the youngest family member at the reunion?
- Who is the oldest family member at the reunion?
- Whose maiden name is HOLDER?

- How many attendees of the reunion have the surname JOHNSTON?
- How many babies under the age of two are at the reunion?
- Where were Grandpa and Grandma WILSON married and when?
- What family group has the most children?

Use your imagination to tailor the questions to the family members in attendance. You might want to omit the age questions, as some family members may be sensitive about revealing their age or having it broadcast. Make copies of your scavenger hunt form and decide when you want to distribute it. Some families include a copy for every family member, along with writing utensils, in the package of materials provided to each family as they arrive at the reunion. Others distribute the materials at the beginning of the first get-together that includes all family members. You will want to give people a deadline for collecting the information. Obviously, if you are hosting a short, one-afternoon event, you will use a short scavenger hunt form; a longer set of questions may be appropriate for a multi-day reunion.

Designate prizes for first, second, and third place winners of the scavenger hunt. Since children and teenagers will love this game, make certain the prizes you select are appropriate for any age group. Theater passes, gift certificates for a fast food restaurant, or small, inexpensive trophies make wonderful prizes.

The "Three New Friends" Game - A variation of the scavenger hunt is the "Three New Friends" game. This game works well at a smaller family get-together as a means of getting people to meet other family members. The goal is to find three people you've never met before, introduce yourselves to one another, and share a different interesting fact about yourself with each person. Give people thirty minutes to make the rounds and meet their new friends. At that time, go around the room and ask people to introduce themselves by name and to introduce their three new friends and tell the whole group the facts that their new friends shared with them. This is a great way for a family group to get to know one another in a more detailed sense rather than just exchanging names and shaking hands. This challenges them to remember names and associate facts with people's faces and then to recount what they've learned. In the process, interesting facts may be revealed that provide some common ground for family members to connect. For example, in one of these games I learned that one cousin shared my interest in working with stained glass, while another cousin and I are deeply involved in genealogical research. If it weren't for this game, I might never have made these connections and begun discussions with them.

Recognition Awards - You might want to consider including a lighthearted and fun presentation ceremony as part of your family reunion. Here you can recognize family members for a variety of reasons. These might include:

- Oldest family member
- Youngest family member
- Person or family who traveled the farthest distance to attend the reunion
- Person or family who traveled the shortest distance to attend the reunion
- Family with the most children
- Family member with the longest (or shortest) hair
- Family member with the longest beard
- Family member with the most freckles

You get the idea. Consider the physical attributes of family members, their achievements, and other criteria in developing a list of lighthearted awards. In addition, this may be the opportunity to recognize family members who have contributed their time and energy to organizing the family reunion and making it happen. You may choose to verbally recognize people or to award them some token gift of esteem.

Tennis Anyone? - Here's a fun physical activity to help people learn others' names and to share information about themselves. Break your family into groups of six or eight people and give each group a tennis ball. Have them toss the ball from one to another around the group. Every time someone catches the ball, he or she has to share a piece of information. For example, the first time someone catches the ball they might say, "My name is Elizabeth." The next time, she might say, "I like to play

classical music on the piano." And the third time, she might reveal that she is a cross-country runner. Let each group spend five minutes or so exchanging information in this manner, and then ask everyone to switch and form new groups. A third time is probably enough for this activity, but you can always use it one more time later in a multi-day reunion to reenergize the group.

"I'm My Own Grandpa" - One way to involve the children in your family in learning more about their ancestors is to host a theme activity. Children love to play dress-up and they love to make up stories. You might consider an "I'm My Own Grandpa" party. This event involves urging the children to learn something about an ancestor. It doesn't have to be a grandfather; it could be a grandmother, a great-grandparent or some other ancestor, and the ancestor does not have to be famous. Encourage the children to gather facts about the ancestor's appearance and life, and to construct a short story about a particular event. They can also be encouraged to create a costume so they can dress for the part. Preparation of the costumes may be one of the children's activities during a multi-day reunion. Set a time for the entire family to gather, and let the children present their stories in costume. Serve cake, cookies, and other refreshments appropriate for a children's party. If you don't want to make this a separate children's event, you might consider incorporating this into some other event, such as a banquet, and let the children provide this as entertainment. You might consider awarding first, second, and third prizes for best story and best costume.

Who's That? - People love to look at photographs. You can create an amusing activity that really gets people talking by compiling a collection of photographs of family members as children. Challenge people to identify the children in the photographs. Start with six to twelve photographs of family members taken when they were between the ages of three and twelve. You can buy an inexpensive bulletin board or a foam display board at any office supply store. You don't want to damage the photographs so consider using plastic sheet protector sleeves for the display. Insert the photographs in the plastic sleeves, attach the sleeves to your display board, and assign numbers to each of the photographs. You can even turn this into a fun and competitive activity by providing forms for people to make their guesses. The form should have a numbered line corresponding with each photograph in your display and a line for the name of the family member submitting the guesses. The activity requires that someone with a master list of correct answers is on hand to review all the guesses submitted. He or she will have to determine which family members came up with the highest number of correct answers. You might declare winners of the top three most accurate guessers and award some small prize, such as a disposable camera.

Secret Word - Some readers may recall the old television show hosted by Groucho Marx called *You Bet Your Life*. At the beginning of that program, a stuffed toy duck was lowered from the ceiling and a secret word was revealed to the audience. In the course of conversation, if one of the contestants used the secret word, he or she won a cash prize. This icebreaker activity is a variation of that concept.

Before the reunion, purchase a package of poker chips and write ordinary words on them using an indelible marking pen. As people arrive at the reunion, give everyone a poker chip and tell them not to reveal the word written on their chip. Once the group has gathered, explain that the goal of the exercise is to meet and talk with as many other family members as possible. The incentive to do so is that a prize will be awarded to the person who collects the most secret words/chips.

To collect a word, a person must say the word in conversation with the person who holds a poker chip with that word. When the word is said, the person holding the chip with a word on it privately shows that chip to the person who said the word. (The emphasis is on privately showing the word on one's chip so that the word stays a secret for use in other conversations.) Each person is on his or her honor and keeps track of his or her own score. The activity continues while people mix and visit with one another so that a large score can be accumulated. At some point, call the group to order and ask for a show of hands to indicate how many secret words they accumulated. ("How many people got five secret words?") Be prepared to award a prize to the person who collected the most secret words. In honor of Groucho Marx and the *You Bet Your Life* show, you might choose a stuffed toy duck as the prize.

Find Yourself – This activity involves posting a genealogical descendants chart in a prominent location and asking people to locate themselves on it. The family genealogist can be a great help in producing such a chart for you. Provide highlighter pens and post a sign instructing family members to highlight their own names on the chart. You will find that people are very

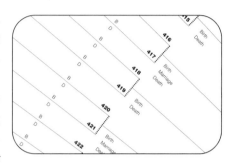

interested in this visual representation of the family and will clamor to locate and highlight their names. The chart can remain posted throughout the reunion and may serve as a reference for everyone to determine which family members are present. You might also consider, in a larger family reunion, setting up a message board. Once people see names highlighted on the descendants chart, they may want to use a message board as a means of making contact with other family members in attendance.

Outdoor Games at Your Reunion – Your family reunion should certainly be a fun and enjoyable event, and games add to the festivities. If your reunion is being held outdoors, you may want to organize games and other activities to take advantage of good weather and fresh air. Most outdoor games will complement a family reunion. Some games requiring little or no equipment you might want to consider are:

- Tag – This classic children's game can be used in situations where there is a lot of free space in which children can run and play.
- Sack race – Adults and children alike can participate in this activity. All you need is sacks.
- Three-legged race – This race only requires an even number of people (you should have at least four) and some rope or cord.
- Hide and go seek – Another classic children's game in which adults can participate as well.
- Blind man's bluff – All you need is a blindfold.

You might consider other organized games such as softball, baseball, basketball, kickball, croquet, badminton, or horseshoes, all of which require sports equipment. However, people can come prepared if you provide them with notice that these activities will take place.

The suggestions in this chapter are only a few ideas, designed to get your creative juices flowing. Use your imagination to come up with icebreaker activities and games that will encourage family interaction, provide fun and enjoyment, and make wonderful memories of your family reunion.

Questions to Ask Yourself ?

- Have we designed the right nametags to help people mix and communicate?

- What games and other icebreaker activities have we chosen or devised to promote communication and interaction?

- Do we have something for all age groups?

- If we have outdoor games planned, who will be the coordinators/facilitators?

- Are there Internet resources that can use to help us plan better activities?

Internet Resources
To Help You Organize Games

Icebreakers

- Family.com: Ways to Reintroduce Everyone: http://family.go.com/Features/
  family_1999_05/famf/famf59reunions/famf59reunions5.html

Games

- Family-Reunion.com: Games for Family Reunions:
  http://familyreunion.com/games.htm
- Family.com: Group Games for Your Reunion:
  http://family.go.com/Features/family_1999_05/famf/famf59reunions/
  famf59reunions9.html
- TOPICS Online Magazine: Children's Games from Around the World:
  http://riceinfo.rice.edu/projects/topics/edition11/games-section.htm

Brady Family Reunion, 1971

Chapter 9

Pursuing Family Genealogy at the Reunion

Reunions are all about family, and any family get-together is an opportunity to share information about the family's history. Reunions actually become a part of your family's ongoing history and tradition. One primary goal of your family reunion should be to promote the sense of belonging to a family, and to help each family member gain a better perspective and appreciation of his or her place in the group.

Most families have at least one person who has an interest in the family's history. He or she usually knows a great deal about names, dates, places, and relationships. This may be a casual interest, or the person may be a dedicated genealogist who has documented the family lineage in substantial detail. If your family is fortunate enough to have more than one of these family historians, the cumulative collaborative effort may have already produced a significant amount of genealogical information.

Your family historian(s) can help you organize this aspect of your family reunion. They can help you coordinate genealogical or family history activities in a number of ways. They usually can produce written materials in the form of pedigree charts, family group sheets, family trees, descendant trees, and other materials appropriate for creating an interesting visual display. They may have historical documents and photographs or may know which family members have similar items in their possession.

Given the opportunity, most family historians will enthusiastically volunteer to help with this aspect of the reunion. It presents an unparalleled opportunity for him or her to collect additional genealogical information about the family. You certainly want to promote any genealogical activity at the reunion as it adds to the collective family knowledge base. Let's discuss some ways to promote the knowledge and sense of family history at your reunion.

In This Chapter

- The importance of sharing family information at a reunion and how it can bring people together

- How to organize a family artifacts display

- How to organize a photographic display

- Gathering genealogical information at the reunion

- Internet resources that can help

Family Artifacts Display - Most families have items in their possession that are considered family treasures, probably passed down from one generation to another. There is usually a story associated with each item. In some families, these treasures may acquire an almost heroic quality over time and the stories associated with the items become cherished family legends. Most, however, retain a mundane quality and reinforce the humanity of their owners. All of these items lend themselves to the construction of a family artifacts display.

Your family reunion is a perfect venue for show-and-tell with family artifacts. You have to make sure, of course, that family members feel comfortable bringing their family treasures and allowing others to see and touch them. This means there should always be careful supervision of the items on display at all times so that nothing is lost or damaged. Every family's collection of treasures is unique, but some items that may be included in your display are:

- Family Bibles
- Framed photographs or portraits
- Letters, deeds, diaries, journals, marriage licenses, and other documents
- Report cards, school books, and compositions
- Great-grandfather's pipe
- Grandmother's wedding or christening dress
- Grandfather's hat or clothing
- Quilts, knitting, embroidery, tatting, and other samples of handwork
- A Civil War sword
- Military medals, ribbons, commendations and other awards
- Farm implements or hand tools
- Kitchen utensils and crockery
- Antique toys

Expensive or valuable items such as clocks, jewelry, and silverware, and fragile items such as china, porcelain, crystal, glassware, pottery, and other breakable items should probably be left at home.

Photographs - Family photographs are always interesting. A display of different family photograph albums can attract a great deal of attention and has the added effect of promoting conversation. People like to share the stories behind their photographs with others and the stories often result in people finding common ground on which to communicate.

Most people have a collection of photographs whose subjects they cannot identify. Another variation of the photographic display allows people to bring their unidentified photographs and ask for help from other family members in identifying them. It is a good idea to have several archive-safe photographic labeling pencils or pens available

for people's use. These can be obtained from many photographic supply companies, office supply stores, or from places on the Web such as Light Impressions Direct <http://www.lightimpressionsdirect.com> or Gaylord <http://www.gaylord.com/archival>. These utensils use acid-free lead and ink components that will not fade or damage the photographic paper or the print images.

As with the artifact display, you will want to have someone supervise the display so nothing is lost or damaged.

Gathering Genealogical Information at the Reunion - Family reunions can be extremely exciting events, especially for a genealogist or family historian. Where else can you get a large group of relatives together and gather so much information at one time? That's the good news. The *not-so-good* news is that you can be overwhelmed with information too.

As always, the key to success is in being organized. Advance preparation is important. Start by gathering all the genealogical information and materials you have collected that are pertinent to the family units involved in the reunion and that you haven't yet completed. That means taking all those photocopies and notes, photographs and vital records, and that mess of sticky notes and going through them. Sort it all out by surname, evaluate it, and enter the appropriate information into your computer database.

Once the data is entered, print new pedigree charts for every branch of the family and every collateral line you think will be represented at the reunion. Prepare these charts for display at the reunion. Take a package of tape flags along so that you can tape the charts to a wall. (The tape flags are less likely to damage a wall than ordinary adhesive tape.) The pedigree charts will be a tremendous hit at the reunion.

In addition to the pedigree charts, print a complete set of family group sheets for all the lines you think will be represented at the reunion. Most genealogical software programs will allow you to print custom reports. I urge you to include on your family group sheets every piece of information you have. That includes dates, notes, and all your source citations. If there is information of which you are unsure or that has yet to be verified or corroborated, you might want to make a notation to that effect so that other family members are aware.

Make several copies of each family group sheet. You might put one complete set in a binder as a master set. You can then write on this set as the reunion takes place and, most importantly, make notes of who told you what. The other sets you can take with you and distribute to key contact people. They can make copies for others in their family and can also update them and return them to you or the family historian.

You will find that people will flock around the family tree display to see what family information has been compiled. Don't get defensive if someone's feathers are ruffled because you have the wrong information. Just explain that the information is what you were told or given, and ask them to give you the correct information and tell you how or where you can find verification. You might want to have a supply of forms and writing utensils handy for people to provide this information on the spot, or you can ask them to mail it to you. A sample form titled Family Genealogy Correction is included here (opposite) as well as in Appendix B.

If you want to collect new information or make corrections to the information you already have, try to enlist one person from each branch of the family or collateral line to act as the coordinator of his or her line. Be prepared to give this person a copy of all the family group sheets for his or her line, as well as some blank copies for new generations or collateral lines. Ask him or her to add to the sheets, make changes or corrections, and

Family Genealogy Correction

Please provide any corrections to the family genealogy by completing the information below. As a conscientious family historian, I try to conduct scholarly and methodical research, and documentation of our family facts is important. Therefore, if you have original materials or copies of documentation that verifies the new/corrected information you are providing below, enclose photocopies for me. I will be happy to reimburse you for the costs of photocopying these materials. Thank you!

Name of individual: _____

What piece of information should be corrected? _____

Information as it appears in the record: _____

New/corrected information: _____

Where is the confirming documentation located? _____

_____

Do you have documentation that can be copied? (Bible records, birth, or death certificates, marriage licenses, wills, deeds, passports, naturalization papers, military records, Social Security information, etc.) _____

_____

_____

Your Name: _____ Tel. #: (____) _____-_____
Address: _____
City: _____ State: _____ ZIP: _____-_____
E-mail Address: _____ @_____

You may mail this to me at:

John Doe
123 Maple Street
Anytown, NY 112233-1018

You can call me with any questions at: (555) 555-5555

My e-mail address is: johndoe@mailserver.net

return them to you. Encourage him or her to also provide you with photocopies of any documents they might have that could verify the information they are providing.

Whatever you do, encourage the return of information to you. Prepare self-addressed 9"x12" manila envelopes with plenty of stamps. Provide an envelope to each person who will be collecting information for you. Tell them that you will reimburse them for any postage and/or photocopies of the additional materials they send to you.

Be prepared to accept all types of information in a variety of formats from your family members. One thing you may want to collect is family recipes. At many family reunions, there are homemade pies, cakes, appetizers, main dishes, and other foods. Some of these recipes have been passed down through the generations; others are new additions to the family traditions. Take some index cards along and compliment the creator by asking him or her for that special recipe.

As for collecting information, I have known people to take a laptop computer to a family reunion for the purpose of displaying information and updating their database on-site. While this *seemed* like a great idea, it actually glued them to the computer and prevented them from circulating, making contacts, asking questions, exchanging information, gathering new information, and otherwise having a great time.

There are four tools I suggest you use to gather information at a family reunion. These are in addition to the family members you enlist to help you update charts and family group sheets. Let's talk about each of the four tools:

- **Steno Pad** - Purchase several steno pads at the office supply store and carry several pens or pencils. As you talk with people and hear interesting stories, ask if you can take notes. Some people may be unnerved by this and refuse so don't press the point. However, listen carefully to what they say, and then jot notes as soon afterward as you can. Whenever you take notes, make sure you indicate who told you what. Like a good journalist, you can always contact the person again later for clarification or more details.

- **Tape Recorder** - A small, handheld cassette tape recorder is an invaluable genealogical tool. I use one whenever I visit a cemetery to read and record the inscriptions on tombstones. If a photo doesn't develop clearly enough to allow me to read the inscription, I still have a record of it on audio tape. At a reunion, a tape recorder is terrific for quickly and accurately capturing information. Always ask permission to tape. Take a number of cassettes with you and label them as you use them. You can assign a number to each cassette and, as you record, make a note on your steno pad of the cassette number, the number of the conversation, and the name of the person you recorded. Be careful not to record over something. Nothing is worse than recording over a wonderful interview! Last but not least, don't forget extra batteries for the recorder.

- **Camera** - A reunion is an invaluable opportunity to take pictures. If you own a camera, make sure you are prepared for all contingencies with all-purpose, indoor/outdoor film. Disposable cameras are inexpensive and versatile, and you may want to take several along. These come in the indoor variety with a built-in flash, the outdoor variety, and in a terrific panorama model that is great for large, wide-angle group shots. Even if you don't use all the film, it is definitely worth the price to obtain those priceless shots.

If you are terrible at remembering names, you may use a technique used by professional photographic journalists. They date and number every roll of film. (You can date and number each disposable camera.) They carry a small pad (like your steno pad) with a date and number at the top of the page corresponding to each of the rolls of film. They number the lines of each page to correspond to each of the pictures on the roll of film. As they take pictures, they make note of the subjects' names (and location if appropriate). Later, when the film is developed, it is easier to identify the people and places in each shot—and the photographer can then correctly label the pictures as needed.

Please note that black-and-white photographs will endure far longer than color shots. You may want to consider taking a roll of black-and-white pictures in addition to color shots for posterity. Digital cameras are also terrific for capturing pictures as data. However, keep in mind that technology changes quickly, and you will need to continue converting your digital photographs to new technologies as they evolve so that the images are never lost to future generations. (Remember 8 mm movies and Beta videotapes?)

- **Video Camcorder** - If you have a video camera, you may want to supplement your genealogical experience by making videotapes. Videos can capture motion pictures, voices, and sounds. They can become a wonderful part of your genealogical collection. Even if there is a professional videographer at your reunion, you may want to make your own videotapes. If you plan to video family members at the reunion, be sure they are not uncomfortable at the prospect. And be sure to ask permission before trying to interview someone on videotape. Take several blank videocassettes with you, and remember the batteries and/or a charger.

All of the above tools can be carried in a shoulder bag. It keeps all your information-gathering tools close at hand and keeps your arms and hands free for important things like hugs, handshakes, and eating all that wonderful food!

Genealogists and family historians at a reunion are like children in a candy store. The opportunities by having so many family members in one place at one time are tremendous, and it is tempting to focus on nothing but gathering information. As a result, genealogists sometimes lose out on the fun and enjoyment of the reunion. If you enlist the help of your family's historian(s), encourage them to participate in the fun and not to relegate themselves strictly to the role of genealogical recorder.

Family Story Time – Another activity that can promote the sharing of family information is a storytelling event. Children love stories, and older adults can use this opportunity to share family stories and traditions with the younger generations. Gather the children together in a quiet spot and let adults share stories from their lives. A great beginning line might be, "Once upon a time, when I was little..."

There are plenty of ways to pursue genealogical research at your family reunion and to share family history with everyone in the group. From the telling of stories to the display of family treasures to the posting of charts and the collection of new and updated family information, everyone can participate in learning about the family's history. And by being part of the family reunion, everyone is participating in building new family traditions.

Questions to Ask Yourself ?

- Who are the family historians or genealogists that can help us promote the sharing of family information?

- What materials can be used to promote learning about our ancestors and our family history?

- Who will coordinate and supervise displays of family artifacts and photographs?

- Will we display family trees, pedigree charts, family group sheets, and other genealogical materials at the reunion? If so, how will we arrange for the displays?

- What methods will we use to collect genealogical information at the reunion and who will do it?

- Are there Internet resources that can help us make the best of genealogical opportunities at the reunion?

Internet Resources

Pursuing Genealogy at Your Family Reunion

The following are links to articles concerning genealogical and family history activities that can be incorporated into your family reunion. All of these and others are available in the Ancestry.com online library <http://www.ancestry.com/learn/main.htm>.

- "Help for Family Reunions" by Juliana Szucs Smith
  http://www.ancestry.com/library/view/news/articles/1841.asp

- "Tips for Planning the Family Reunion" by George G. Morgan
  http://www.ancestry.com/library/view/columns/george/848.asp

- "Family Reunions and Old Photographs" – Ancestry Quick Tip by Bonnie Knutson – http://www.ancestry.com/library/view/news/tip/261.asp

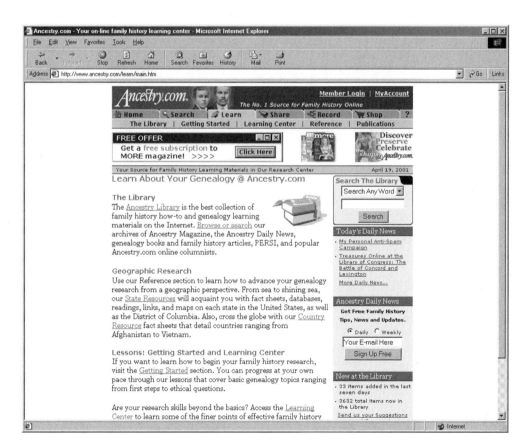

Cox Family Reunion, date unknown.

Chapter 10

Managing Details at the Reunion

Most of the activities at a family reunion will take care themselves. People will usually pitch in and help with whatever needs to be done, and you can usually enlist people's help as needed. Some of the logistical details, however, will need to be supervised. In this chapter, let's discuss some suggestions for managing these types of details at the reunion. Your list may be longer or shorter, depending on the size and type of reunion you are hosting.

In This Chapter

- How to keep track of where people are at the reunion
- How to create and effectively use signs
- How to make announcements and use newsletters
- The importance of double-checking everything
- Evaluating the success of the reunion
- Internet resources that can help

Locating People

It can be important to know how to locate people at your reunion. This is especially true if your event is being held at a hotel or resort. If you ask in advance, the hotel will usually designate a block of rooms for your party. This keeps your group together and can make the logistics of communicating with everyone much simpler. You can also ask the hotel staff for a list of the members of your group and the rooms in which they are staying.

If your reunion is held somewhere other than a hotel, you still want to be able to locate people. You might want to use a sign-in sheet or a guest book, asking families to sign in as they arrive. This serves two purposes. First, it allows anyone to check to see who is in attendance. Second, it is a written record of the attendance at the event, while also providing the family genealogist with handwriting samples.

I have attended larger reunions where there were sign-up sheets used for various activities, such as softball games, swimming, and hikes. These activities always involved at least one adult as the facilitator whose job it was to get a complete list of participants and get it back to a central point at the reunion. This made it possible to know where specific individuals were in the event they needed to be found. While this may seem like extra work, it is essential to keep track of children who might wander off and not be missed for some time.

An added bonus to the use of sign-up sheets is that they provide a record for the reunion planners of the popularity of specific activities. This information can be helpful in planning more of the same or different activities at subsequent reunions.

Signage

Regardless of the type of reunion, you will probably use signs or bulletin boards to help your family members find the right place for each event. If you follow the suggestions in previous chapters, you will have given thought to and prepared a number of signs.

Signs used outdoors should be constructed with weatherproof materials, should use bright colors, and should have lettering that is large enough to be read at a distance. It's always better to have more signs than less.

Signs intended for indoor use can be of several types. Consider using stiff poster board stock and displaying them on easels. In a hotel or conference center, easels are readily available and provide flexibility of placement. Larger signs near the entrance in the lobby and near the exit to a parking garage can announce the name of the reunion and its location inside the facility. Similar or smaller signs can be used at the entrance to the place where an event will actually be held. Smaller signs can be prepared with a computer and posted at or near the entrance.

Signage is an important part of your crowd management at the reunion. Therefore, be prepared to post the signs well in advance of anyone's anticipated arrival at the event. Consider placing the signs one or more hours before the event begins.

As discussed earlier in the book, if your reunion is being held at a hotel, work with the staff to post your events on hotel bulletin boards and electronic signs. Be sure to prepare your schedule of events and their locations and deliver it in advance to your hotel contact person. This will help ensure that he or she has ample time to review and post the announcements. In addition, provide him or her extra copies of the schedule and request that they be given to the hotel operator and the front desk. They will then have information at their fingertips in the event that someone asks for information or directions.

If you use a registration and/or information table for your group, make certain that the people working there have copies of the schedule. They also should know where each event is to be held so they can give directions. They should also have extra copies on hand for people who have lost or misplaced their schedule or who have left it in their hotel room.

Announcements and Newsletters

Some families hosting multi-day reunions prepare flyers or newsletters for distribution on-site. Flyers provide an excellent way to communicate changes in your preprinted schedule or to announce impromptu events. Newsletters published at the reunion can add a lot of fun and excitement to the event. They can perform the same function as flyers, but they can also broadcast news of events at the reunion. For example, I prepared the shells of three newsletters for one of our family reunions. Each

Weatherly Reunion News

Day 3 ~ Saturday, June 2, 2001

GOOD MORNING!

It's going to be a GREAT day at the reunion today! What better place to enjoy yourself than here in the cradle of our family tree -- Rome, GA. There are lots of wonderful events planned for the day that will give us a chance to get to know one another and renew our relationships. Here is today's schedule:

8:00-10:00 AM - Breakfast at Emma Dale Holder's home at 104 East Sixth Avenue

10:30 AM - Relaxation by the hotel pool

Noon-1:30 PM - Pizza party for the younger set (to age 18) in the Roman Room at the Forrest Hotel

Noon - Everyone else is on their own for lunch

2:00-5:00 PM - Softball, badminton and croquet at Heritage Park (see map in your packet)

2:00-4:00 PM - Walking tour of Myrtle Hill Cemetery

5:00-6:30 PM - Our Family Pictures and Heirlooms Exhibition and Family Genealogy Display - Roman Room at the Forrest Hotel

6:30-8:30 PM - Reunion Banquet in the Grand Ballroom at the Forrest Hotel The kids will stage their "I'm My Own Grandpa/Grandma" show

8:30-11:00 PM - Dancing in the Grand Ballroom with entertainment provided by DJ "Cool Eddie" Masterson

10:00-Midnight - Late night snacks available in the Bell Tower Cafe

---

Pick Up Your Reunion T-shirts

If you ordered a T-shirt for this reunion, they are available from 9:00 AM to 5:00 PM at our registration/information desk in the Forrest Hotel lobby. Pick yours up and wear it with pride today!

OUR FAMILY FOUNDERS

Walton & Elizabeth Holder Weatherly's Wedding Day - September 16, 1908 - Rome, Georgia
(Copies of picture can be ordered from Cousin George.)

Reunion Banquet

Your presence is requested at the Weatherly Family Banquet at 6:30 o'clock this evening in the Grand Ballroom of the Forrest Hotel.

Pizza Party!

Kids of all ages! Join us in the hotel's Roman Room for a pizza party from Noon to 1:30 today! Great food! Prizes! Special entertainment just for you!

newsletter contained stories of general interest that I had written in advance of the reunion. At the end of each day, I wrote recaps of that day's events and inserted them into the shell document for that day. I then printed the newsletter and took it to a 24-hour photocopy service where I had it copied and stapled. Early the next morning, using the list obtained from the hotel of family members and their room numbers, two of us slid copies of the daily newsletter under people's doors. The response was terrific!

Announcement fliers and newsletters can be prepared in advance, or they can be created, printed, and copied locally if someone has a portable computer and printer, or if a family member with such equipment lives close by. Keep in mind that hotels charge a premium rate for their photocopy services. You will therefore want to find a local photocopying service near the hotel.

Arrival and Sign-In

The culmination of your advance planning for registrations comes when your family members arrive at the reunion. At a minimum, you want to provide everyone with a nametag. You may have prepared these in advance with a computer or you may allow people to create their own using a felt tip pen and a blank nametag.

Your reunion may consist of many activities, so you may therefore want to prepare an attendee packet for each family or individual. A typical attendee packet might consist of:

- A large envelope labeled with the family or person's name
- Nametag(s) - One for each day, blank or pre-printed, for every person
- Schedule of events and locations
- List of other attendees or family contact directory
- Information about purchasing or picking up commemorative items
- Information about ordering or purchasing photographs and/or videotapes to be made during the reunion
- Map of the hotel, conference center, park or other facility
- Map of the area
- Brochures about local attractions

In addition to the list above, you may have specific materials that are unique to specific attendees. These might include a receipt for a last-minute registration, tickets and transportation information for only those people who arranged in advance to participate in a group excursion, a personal note, or some other unique item. By having an attendee packet customized with a family unit's name, you can provide a unique and comprehensive packet of materials to your attendees. All these packets should be prepared in advance of the reunion. They can be filed alphabetically by name in cardboard boxes or plastic egg crates for ease of transport and access.

Set up a registration and sign-in table near the entrance to the reunion area. In a hotel or conference center, you can usually set it up in the lobby. Have a list of all expected attendees available so their names can be checked off as they arrive. Have all your materials and supplies ready. This includes the pre-assembled attendee packets, extra schedules, pens and pencils, tape, scissors, paper clips, rubber bands, nametags, and markers. In addition, make sure you have people's original registration forms available in case there are any questions about who registered and paid in advance for whom and what.

If you are distributing commemorative merchandise, decide on a procedure in advance that includes where and when the distribution will occur. If you are distributing something like T-shirts or caps that people will wear at the reunion, you might consider having them available when family members arrive at the registration desk. Have the cartons behind the registration desk and already organized, if appropriate, by color and size. This will streamline the process of locating sized merchandise and distributing it.

If you are distributing things like coffee mugs or other items at a banquet, consider placing one at each plate at the dining tables. This advance work eliminates the need for people to work at distributing the items while others are enjoying the meal.

Hospitality Events

Your reunion at a hotel or resort may include one or more hospitality events, such as the first-night reception or cocktail party for the adults and a games mixer for the children. These are usually informal events but there is always potential for problems. About thirty minutes in advance, check the facility to make sure it is set up correctly. Beverages, cups and

glasses, and ice should already be there. Non-perishable food items may also be present but other hot and cold items will probably be brought in just before the start of the event. If there appears to be a problem, immediately go to the front desk and ask for your contact person. He or she will be able to get things on track.

Banquets and Other Food Events

Food is a very important component of a family reunion and there are all types of food events. Your reunion may center around a picnic or cookout in a park or a family potluck dinner to which people bring covered dishes. In these cases, it is important to coordinate the details of who brings what. You may otherwise end up with fifteen bags of potato chips and no main course. For the more simple family events, you will probably have asked relatives to sign up in advance to bring specific items. On the day of the event, have the list handy as people arrive with their contributions to the meal. Check each item off as it arrives. As you do so, you may quickly recognize that some people may not have brought the dish to which they committed. Catching these changes and omissions early enough may allow time for quick a run to the grocery store to fill the gap.

Many reunions include a formal banquet. As we discussed earlier in the book, planning for such an affair requires a substantial amount of effort. It involves coordinating the arrangements for a banquet room, decorations, catering, entertainment, photographer and videographer, and any number of other details. Each of these areas presents an opportunity for disaster. If you did your advance work correctly, you will have made contact with each of the individuals responsible for his or her respective aspects of your banquet in the week prior to the event. You will have confirmed the numbers of attendees and all the arrangements. After doing so, you will have done as much as possible in advance to guarantee the success of the event.

At least an hour prior to your banquet, check the banquet room to ensure that tables, chairs, place settings and any other materials are set up properly. Inspect the room for any signs of existing damage. If any new damage is noted since you performed your walk-through, notify your hotel contact immediately and ask him or her to come to the banquet room. This small action can prevent big charges later.

Check the room to see that signs, decorations, displays, and any floral arrangements are in place. The caterer or hotel food service people should have arrived and begun their set-up work. Ask to see and sample the food. Be alert for any substitutions.

Any entertainment you may have engaged should also have arrived and begun setting up. It is important that lighting and sound checks be done prior to the banquet so they don't interrupt the event. Photographers and videographers should also arrive in advance to discuss any last minute instructions with you.

Remember that these people are working for you and are there to perform a service that they agreed to in a contract. Never assume that everything will run perfectly. A last-minute run-through with these individuals will ensure that they understand precisely what is expected. Don't be concerned that they think you are obsessive. Your attention to the details immediately prior to the banquet will keep them focused and help ensure the success of the event.

Transportation

If your reunion involves the transportation of people from one location to another, and you contracted with a transportation company, you will need to keep track of all the details. You should have confirmed the date, location, and numbers of people to be transported with the carrier just prior to the event. You also should have verified the arrival time. This advance follow-up work will help guarantee that the right accommodations are available when you need them.

Prepare in advance a list of names of all family members who will be making the trip. Prior to departure, someone should be responsible for checking off the names as people board the vehicle. This ensures that everyone who signed up is there and that others who may not have signed up or paid have the opportunity to do so.

The vehicle you engaged should arrive to pick up passengers at the agreed-upon time. Be prepared with the contact name and telephone number of the transportation company in the event the vehicle does not arrive on time.

Cleanup

Make sure you understand your responsibility for cleaning up the place where you hold your family reunion. If you use a park, your group is generally responsible for policing the area and placing any garbage into proper receptacles. Camp fires and barbecue grills must be completely extinguished. A good rule of thumb is to leave the area

in as good or better shape than you found it.

A reunion held at a hotel or resort may be a different situation. Your contractual agreement should be clear regarding responsibility for cleanup. The hotel is typically responsible for cleaning its own facility, but you will probably be responsible for the removal and disposal of any decorations and floral arrangements you provided. The catering company should be responsible for removing its equipment and for cleaning up after itself.

The hotel may impose a cleaning surcharge for anything beyond its normal responsibilities. Therefore, it is a good idea for someone to remain in the banquet room to make sure that everything is cleaned up properly and that nothing is damaged in the process.

Evaluations

One the most important ways to determine the success of your family reunion is to ask family members to complete an evaluation. It is in the evaluation that you can learn specifically what you did right and what areas need improvement. You may opt to ask everyone to complete an evaluation or only asking the heads of families to do so on their family's behalf. You might even choose a random evaluation sampling of family members. You will find a sample evaluation form included in the next chapter, as well as in Appendix B of this book. Your evaluation form will vary depending on the size and type of reunion you host, and will probably be different than the one included in this book. However, feel free to use this sample as a basis for designing your own form. You may decide to include your evaluation in the attendee packet so that people know from the outset that you will be seeking feedback. Or you may pass it out at the end of the reunion. Whatever you do, however, you definitely want feedback about every aspect of the reunion. Only in this way can you learn how to do it better the next time.

?

Questions to Ask Yourself

- How can we keep track of where people are at the reunion?

- What kinds of signs will we need, what should be on them, and where will we place them?

- Will we need to make any announcements or communicate on-site? If so, how will we do that?

- Have we identified what things need to be double-checked and who will do the checking?

- What clean-up will we be responsible for, how will we organize that, and who will do the work?

- Have we created an evaluation form? How will we distribute it and collect it?

Internet Resources
To Help You Evaluate the Success of Your Reunion

• Hall of Names International, Inc.'s Family Reunion Evaluation Form - Web page containing a variety of reunion-related registration, including a sample evaluation form. http://www.myroots.com/reunion.htm

• FormalSoft, Inc.'s Family-reunion.com Evaluation Form - Online family reunion evaluation form. http://family-reunion.com/evaluate.htm

In addition, you can use your favorite Internet search engine(s) to locate evaluation forms created by other families for their reunions. Appendix A describes in detail how to effectively structure this type of search on the Web.

Browser window — family-reunion.com - Family reunion evaluation form - Microsoft Internet Explorer

Address: http://www.family-reunion.com/evaluate.htm

Family Reunion Evaluation Form

Entering your name is optional if required to express your true feelings

Name_____
Address_____
City_____ State_____ Postal code_____
Country_____ New address? ___Yes ___No
Phone_____ Email_____
Website_____

General feelings about this years reunion

Did you enjoy the reunion this year? ___Yes ___No ___Mixed feelings
Would you attend another reunion next year? ___Yes ___No ___Depends

What did you like or dislike about this years reunion?

Did you like where the reunion was held? ___Yes ___No
  Why or why not?_____
How was the reunion length? ___Too long ___Too short ___Just right
How was the number of activities? ___Too many ___Too few ___Just the right amount
What was your **favorite** activity?_____
What was your **least** favorite activity?_____
Did you like the food? ___Yes ___No ___Some of it ___Most of it
  Which food would you **not** have again?_____
What one thing should we definitely do again next year? _____

If you could change one thing about the reunion, what would it be? _____

Do you have any suggestions for future reunions?

How long should the reunion be? ___ 1 afternoon ___ weekend ___long weekend
Location ideas_____
Best time of year

Done   Internet

Wright Family Reunion, 1965

After the Ball...

Your family reunion is over and the results are in. Most family members will have completed the evaluation of the event and given you their opinions. Almost everyone will have enjoyed it, but there will invariably be a few people who will pan all or portions of the event. You probably can't please everyone, but you certainly want to try. Keep an open mind when reviewing your evaluations. You want to honestly accept criticism of this year's get-together and suggestions for changes and improvements in future reunions.

As soon after the reunion as possible, while it is still fresh in your mind, make notes of what went right and what went wrong. Ideally, the time to make these notes is at the end of the reunion day, but you may be too exhausted to do so. However, don't delay. These impressions are important.

Likewise, take the time to summarize the results of the evaluations as soon as possible. To do so, make a question-by-question list, tally the results of 1-5 ratings etc., and transcribe the comments. At the conclusion of this exercise, you will have all your evaluation material in one document.

Next, ask the treasurer to prepare a final accounting report of income and expenses. This is a crucial document because, if there is any shortfall, you will immediately need to determine how to cover that expense. Hopefully this won't be necessary but, if so, you may have to go back to family members and ask for additional money to cover it. If there is any profit, these funds may be placed in the family reunion bank account and set aside as seed money for a future reunion. Otherwise, you might consider refunding money to attendees.

The next step is to make copies of the evaluation summary and the final accounting report. Get copies to key members of the planning committee and schedule a meeting

Family Reunion Evaluation

The reunion planning team worked hard to put together a fun and enjoyable event for the family. We know there are always things we could do to make the next reunion better and would like your feedback. Your name is optional.

Name: (optional) _____

How did you like the location where the reunion was held?

_____

_____

Should we consider the same place or something like it next year?   YES   NO

If NO, where would you suggest we hold our next reunion and what kind of facility should we consider?

_____

_____

On a scale of 1 to 5, with a 5 being the best, how would you rate the meals? _____

Was there something you really liked or disliked about the meals?

_____

_____

What was your favorite event at the reunion? _____

What was your *least* favorite event at the reunion? _____

On a scale of 1 to 5, with a 5 being the best, how would you rate the overall reunion?_____

What aspects of the reunion would you like us to keep next time? _____

_____

What improvements or changes would you like to see made for the next reunion?

_____

_____

Would you be willing to help plan and organize the next reunion?   YES   NO

If YES, please list your name and telephone number:
Name: _____ Telephone: (___) _____ - _____

THANK YOU FOR TAKING THE TIME TO GIVE US YOUR FEEDBACK

to discuss them. This *post mortem* is an important step in the process because it brings together the impressions and opinions of both the planning team *and* the reunion attendees. It gives you an opportunity to assess how effective your planning and organization process was, which activities worked and which did not, and allows you to determine what changes and improvements you could make for future reunions. Hopefully, your evaluations were full of kudos and calls for more reunions in the future.

Now is the time for you and your team members to begin planning the next reunion. The review that the group performs should be documented. Make notes for the next reunion team. Everyone involved in this year's reunion will have learned from the experience. One great contribution each team member can make is to document each of the activities they handled in their area of responsibility and the steps they took to fulfill their obligations. They should document the steps that worked and the pitfalls they encountered that might be avoided. You might consider creating a binder with tab binders labeled for the various areas of responsibility and file the write-ups for reference by the next reunion team. Be sure to include copies of all the contracts as samples and make notes of any problems caused by the terms of the contract or by any omissions.

Another extremely important post-reunion activity involves thanking the members of your reunion planning and organization team. Without their help, you never would have been able to put together a successful reunion. Although you may have publicly recognized these people at the reunion, a personalized thank-you letter is always appreciated. It goes a long way toward compensating them for the time and energy they volunteered, and is another way to encourage them to participate in planning future reunions.

Family Reunion Evaluation Summary

Question	Responses		Comments
Liked Location	YES	32 people	People liked having reunion in hometown
	NO	2 people	Was too far to travel
	NEUTRAL	1 person	Hard traveling with children
Same Place Next Year?	YES	24 people	"There's nothing like coming home!"
	NO	9 people	Would like to do something different.
	NEUTRAL	2 people	Would like reunion closer to west coast folks
Different Place Next Year?	YES	5 people	Suggestions included Disney World,
	NO	25 people	Yosemite Park and Chicago
	NEUTRAL	5 people	
How Were Meals? (Ratings based in 1 being poor and 5 being terrific)	5	18 people	Banquet got good reviews overall
	4	10 people	"Great breakfasts with the relatives."
	3	5 people	Kids loved the pizza party
	2	0 people	One person said the desserts weren't good
	1	2 people	
Favorite Event			Games and food events were the favorites
Least Favorite Event			Nobody responded to this question
Overall Reunion Rating (Ratings based in 1 being poor and 5 being terrific)	5	18 people	Banquet got good reviews overall
	4	10 people	"Great breakfasts with the relatives."
	3	5 people	Kids loved the pizza party
	2	0 people	One person said the desserts weren't good
	1	2 people	
Aspects to be Kept			Banquet, games, pizza party, family displays
Suggested Changes			More leisure time to visit, better desserts
Willing to Help Next Time			7 new people volunteered for next year

Martin Family Newsletter

Vol. 6 No. 3

Your Cousin Joseph is No Ordinary Joe

BY JOY HARRIS

From the time he was just a boy, Joseph Martin (Judy Martin's second son) knew just what he wanted to do with his life: He wanted to sing.

His many hours of practice, starting with voice lessons at age four, have paid off. Last March, Joseph was named first tenor of the St. Louis Opera.

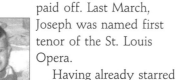
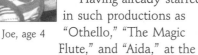

Joe, age 4

Having already starred in such productions as "Othello," "The Magic Flute," and "Aida," at the Duluth Community Repertory Theatre by the time he was 15, Joseph, now just 18, is prepared to star in the region's largest opera company. But it

see Joseph, p. 3

Don't forget Grandma Martin's birthday August 15. She would love to hear from you on her special day.
Her phone number is (555) 555-5555

ANCESTRAL HOME: Here we see great-grandfather Jonas Martin with his extended family on the occasion of a family get-together. Notice how men and women are walking down different paths.

Family News

• The Annual Martin family reunion was a smash success. Thanks to all who participated with the food and different activities. Special thanks goes to Judy Martin who headed up this year's reunion committee. See you at next year's reunion!

• Ja Nae Matthews (grand-daughter of Constance Martin) has been awarded a cooking scholarship to the Betty Crocker University located in Minneapolis, MN.

• John Martin has gotten a job in New York City, and is in need of a place to stay in the city until he can find an apartment. Anyone with information can contact John directly at (555) 555-5566.

• Grandma Martin's surgery went great, and she is back home in time for her birthday celebration (August 15, at her home).

Looking toward the Next Reunion

Just because this year's family reunion is done doesn't mean you can let the grass grow under your feet. It will soon be time to plan the next reunion. You will want to help the family "keep the feeling" so they will be enthusiastic about the next one. One way to do that is to prepare and mail a newsletter recapping the event. You can include the names of everyone who attended, descriptions of the activities, photographs from the banquet and other events, and family news. Who knows? The newsletter might become a regularly published communication vehicle for the family and therefore another means of publicizing the next reunion. Send a copy of the newsletter to every family unit, including the family members who did not attend the reunion. Seeing what they missed may encourage them to attend the next time.

Another way to help the family "keep the feeling" is to create and/or maintain an Internet-based family site. As we discussed in Chapter 6, MyFamily.com offers a free Web-based facility where you can create your family's own terrific Web site. Located at <http://www.myfamily.com>, you can publish family news, add and display photographs, create an online family address book, set up a calendar with birth dates and anniversaries (and family reunions!), add your family's genealogical information, and host online family chats. And with the use of free, downloadable software, you can talk with one another over the Internet just as you might via telephone. The MyFamily.com Web site offers a comprehensive online environment that fosters communication and information sharing between family members. Access is private and limited to only those family members you invite to enter and view your data. MyFamily.com is a unique facility that you and your family can use for year-round communication.

Your reunion planning has been a success. You have brought your family members together for a celebration of the clan. The new relationships that were formed and the existing ones that were strengthened reinforce the unity of your family. Every opportunity in which the family can be brought together and reunited is priceless. You have succeeded in giving a priceless gift to your family—the sense of belonging to family.

Congratulations on your very successful family reunion!

? Questions to Ask Yourself

- What will we do with the information from the reunion evaluations?

- Who will summarize and review the data?

- What did we do well that people liked? What did we do that people didn't like? What could we have done better?

- What improvements can we make for the next reunion?

- How did we do with the finances? Were we over or under our budget? What do we do with any leftover money, or how do we cover the shortfall?

- Have we thanked everyone who helped?

- How do we start planning our next successful family reunion?

Appendix A

Family Reunion Resources on the Internet

The Internet has changed the way we communicate and exchange information forever. Since the first graphical Web browser was introduced in 1993, businesses and individuals have surged forward to publish materials on the World Wide Web (WWW) in the form of Web pages. Today, it is estimated that there are almost 1.5 billion distinct Web page addresses, and that number increases by the thousands every day.

Throughout this book, I have included Internet addresses of useful resources for your family reunion planning. I focused on high-quality sites that have been around for a good while and that should have some longevity on the Web. Because of the nature of the medium, however, few Internet sites are guaranteed to remain unchanged. Web sites come and go, and sometimes a Web address may change without its administrator or webmaster providing a link redirecting you to the new site. And sometimes a Web site just disappears, a casualty of a lack of interest, time, or funding.

The Web addresses in the chapters of this book provide links to specific Internet resources. Every reunion is, of course, unique, and you will want to locate Web sites to help you achieve specific goals. You may be looking for a vendor in your area to create your commemorative T-shirt or coffee mug, or you may want to locate information on a cruise to Cozumel. With all the information on the Internet today, there is little doubt that you can find exactly the right information to help you make your reunion an unqualified success.

If you have been using the Internet for a while, you probably know about search engines. These powerful online tools index data on Web pages and can be used to search for keywords and/or phrases to locate Web sites that match the information you seek. If you haven't used search engines, it's time to learn how to harness their power to

In This Appendix

- Search engines and directories and how to use them.

- Structuring effective searches on the Internet

- Fine-tuning your searches

- Publishing your family reunion on the Web

- Internet resources that can help

search the Web. Regardless of your level of experience or expertise, this appendix will provide you with a clearer understanding of how to locate Web-based materials to help with your reunion planning.

What Is a Search Engine?

Search engines are powerful tools for searching the Internet (most often the Web) for information using keywords and phrases. There are really two search entities on the Web—directories and search engines—and it is important to understand the distinction between the two in order to understand what each one can provide.

A directory is a compilation of Web addresses and descriptive information arranged into categories and subcategories, something like a reference library. Directories are compiled by human beings and represent someone's conscious decision to include (or exclude) a particular Web site in the directory and place it in a specific category. The largest and most successful directory is Yahoo! at <http://www.yahoo.com>. Yahoo! provides the ability to search its own contents.

Directories are organized into categories, subcategories, and sub-subcategories. From the main screen of a directory such as Yahoo!, you can click on a category and a new screen will be displayed showing all the subcategories. Click on one of these and a screen displaying subcategories is displayed. This hierarchical structure is helpful in locating information on specific topics. Most directories also cross-reference materials in other hierarchical categories you may not have considered. For example, in the example shown below, in the main category of Recreation, there are twenty-two sub-categories displayed.

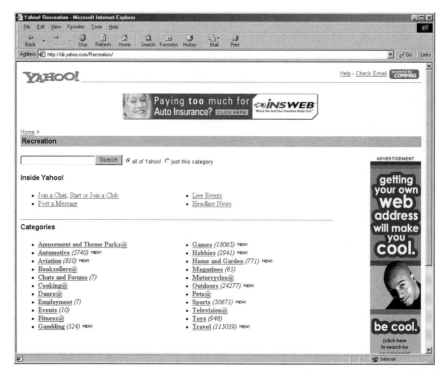

The sub-subcategories are listed with numbers in parentheses. These numbers indicate the number of items you would find within that sub-subcategory were you to click on that link. If you click on the link to Games, with its 17,824 items, you will be presented with another screen with items and more categories. At the top of the screen you will notice a line that looks like the image below:

The Home>Recreation> line is actually a series of links indicating the hierarchical structure into which you have navigated. Therefore, we have moved from the Yahoo! Home page to the Recreation category, and now we are in the Games subcategory, as indicated by the horizontal bar labeled "Games."

You may have noticed along the way that there are other items listed with the @ sign at the end. The @ sign indicates a cross-reference link to another hierarchical categorical structure within Yahoo!. If, for example, you went back to the Recreation category and clicked on the link labeled Pets@, you would find yourself on a screen whose hierarchical list would be as shown below:

Navigating through a directory site is fine *if you know where to look*. In some cases, though, it is easier to use the directory site's search facility and locate all the resources. In the case of Yahoo!, you can search from its home page or from any of the subsidiary category pages. In the latter case, you can specify whether to search only that category or all of Yahoo!, as shown below:

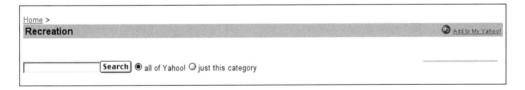

A full search of Yahoo! will display a list of results from the category, followed by a list of results from other areas, complete with links to the hierarchical lists where the results were found. All of these are clickable to help you quickly and efficiently navigate directly to the results. In addition, Yahoo! presents lists of links to other Web sites. If Yahoo! finds no matches in its own directory listings, it reverts to an external search engine and uses that engine to locate matches on the Internet.

A search engine is a different kind of Internet tool. It is an indexed compilation of Web pages collected from the Internet by electronic scouts known as robots, bots, or spiders. Web page content is indexed by search engines using three key components of a Web page:

The Title - The title of a Web page is created and assigned by the author of the Web page. The title is what appears in the title bar at the top of your Web browser window. (Do not confuse this with the heading in the content area of the Web page.)

META Tags - META tags are keywords defined by the Web page's author to help search engines index the page. A Web page about Native Americans might have META tags added for the terms Indian, Sioux, Cherokee, and so on. The META tag keywords themselves are not visible when you are viewing the Web page; they are hidden in the background and are seen only if you use your browser's View Source facility to see the HTML code used to write the Web page. You should be aware that some Web authors attempt to force their Web pages to come up higher in a search engine's ranking scheme by repeating the same keyword multiple times in their META tags.

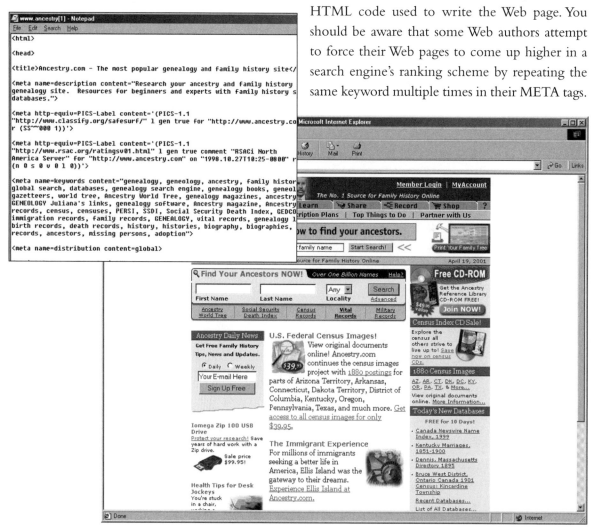

The search engines are wise to this and, on encountering this "spam factor," may ignore multiple uses of that keyword or ignore and bypass the META tags altogether.

Page Content - The text on every page and the file names of included graphics, sounds, and videos are indexed. So-called "stopper" words, such as articles (the, a, etc.), conjunctions (and, either, or, neither, nor), prepositions (of, for, by, etc.), and punctuation marks are ignored.

The resultant information is indexed into a searchable database that is used whenever you issue a search against the search engine's content. You should be aware that no search engine indexes the entire Web. Even the largest search engines, such as Google, Alta Vista, and Fast Search, index only a portion of the Web. Some Web sites block search engines' robots or spiders from accessing their sites to index them. As a result, a very significant percentage of Web pages at such sites as America Online, CompuServe, and at colleges, universities, and many corporations may never be indexed. In addition, information in searchable databases at other Web sites are not accessible for indexing by a search engine. You would need to visit that Web site and use its own online search function in order to access the contents of its database.

The Best Search Engines

There are more than twenty major search engines that can be used to search the Web. There are others that specialize in searching news services, financial news, or other areas. All of the major ones are free to use. Several factors differentiate search engines from one another. These include:

Area of Focus - Some search engines index Web content regardless of what the content may be, while others focus more on mass media or other types of content.

Relevancy Ranking - This is the way the search engine interprets the keyword or phrase you enter, searches its index, and arranges the matches for presentation back to you. The matches are arranged in some order based on the logic of the engine's program based on what it believes is relevant to the data you entered. A search for the word "reunion" in two search engines may yield some of the same *and different* matches, and the ones that they have in common may be presented in a different relevancy ranking order. Some of the search engines even display a percentage to indicate how relevant their indexing software calculated each match to be to the keyword or phrase you entered.

Frequency of Update - Search engines vary in the frequency at which their indexes are refreshed. Some are updated weekly and others are updated as seldom as once a month. Some purge "dead" links (the sites that are no longer active) as part of their refresh processing, while others do so less frequently or never at all.

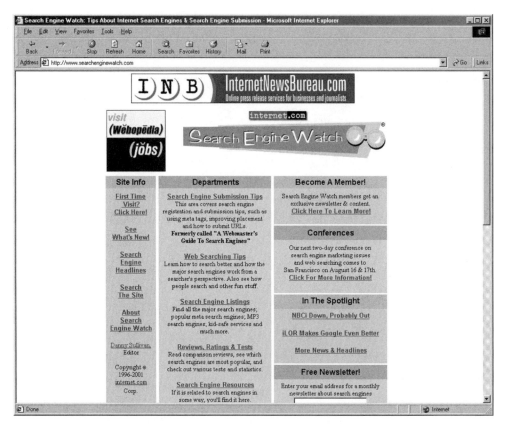

You will want to determine which search engine(s) you like best and learn how to use them effectively. The best place to learn about search engines is at a Web site called Search Engine Watch, located at <http://www.searchenginewatch.com>. This site tracks of all the major search engines, monitors changes in the amount of the Web each one indexes, rates and ranks them, and provides excellent help for learning how to use them. Its tutorials and Web Searching Tips, at <http://www.searchenginewatch.com/facts/index.html>, will teach you how to effectively use search engines, structure searches to find the information you want, and control your searches to hone in on specific resources, especially those that will help you with your family reunion planning.

Among the best search engines available today are:

- Google - http://www.google.com
- FastSearch - http://www.alltheweb.com
- Alta Vista - http://www.altavista.com
- HotBot - http://www.hotbot.com
- LookSmart – http://www.looksmart.com

Using a Search Engine

Search engines are easy to use. Simply enter the URL of the search engine in your Web browser, press enter, and wait for its Web page to load. Once there, you're presented with a small window in which you can type the word(s) for which you wish to search. Type the word and press enter. The search engine will look through its database and present you with a search results list. The list will contain matches and, as discussed before, will be ordered in some relevancy ranking sequence. In other words, the search engine will determine relevant matches to the word(s) or phrase you entered, and will rank the results from highest to lowest relevancy.

When you are entering keywords in a search engine, always enter them in lower case. Do not use any capital letters. Search engines are programmed to accept capitalized words or words typed in all upper case letters and look for exact matches. That means that if you type the word "REUNION," the search engine would not find any Web pages where the word is typed as either "reunion" or "Reunion." However, if you type your search word in all lower case, the search engine will look for reunion, REUNION, and any variations of upper and lower case and any mixed case.

In addition, always enter keywords in the singular, not plural. If, for example, you were searching for information about mockingbirds, enter "mockingbird." A search engine will search for matches to "mockingbird" *and* "mockingbirds." If you entered "mockingbirds," the search engine would only return Web pages containing the plural version of the word and you would miss other sites containing the singular version of "mockingbird."

You can review the search results list and click on various links to go to those Web sites to review their Web page content. If the search results list seems too large or too broad, you can revise your search to narrow it down. One way of doing that is with a Boolean search. What's that? Well, English mathematician George Boole developed a means of evaluating materials on a simple true-false scale using certain conditions. You'll perhaps remember this from your math classes. You evaluate materials based on the use of AND, OR, and NOT. Some search engines will also support proximity of words to one another using NEAR. Let's look at an example.

Let's say you were searching for information about T-shirts for your family reunion. At the time of this writing, I used the Google search engine and entered the following information (in all lower case) in its simple search area:

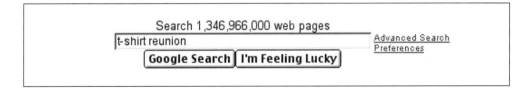

Search engines assume that, if you enter two words, you want it to search for Web pages that contain both words, i.e., they assume the use of the AND Boolean operator. In this case, Google returned 20,700 matches, with the supposedly most-relevant matches listed first. (They also included some paid advertising or "sponsored links" at the top of the list.) Among the links were Web sites related to reunions and T-shirts.

Twenty thousand links are *a lot* to wade through. I then decided I wanted to narrow my search to T-shirts for family reunions.

You can force a search engine to treat multiple words as a phrase and look for matches where the words are in precise adjacency to one another. To do this, you simply enclose the words in quotes, as shown in the following example:

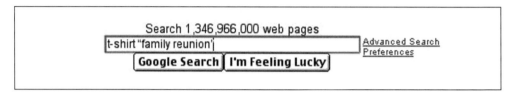

In this case, I wanted to locate Web pages containing both the word "t-shirt" and the phrase "family reunion" (keep in mind that usage of upper, lower, or mixed case varies with each search engine). This time, the matches Google returned were different. There were 3,120 matches and the top ten were a somewhat different batch.

Search engines most frequently support the use of Boolean searches in their *advanced search* facilities. When you go to most search engine Web sites, their *simple search* facility is presented first. You have to click on a link to another page to use the advanced facility. Take the time to read its "Help" or "Search Tips." These can help you quickly understand what search options its search engine supports and how to effectively structure your search to optimize your use of the engine.

In the advanced area, you might want to further narrow your search by specifying that you want Web pages containing the word "t-shirt" and the phrase "family reunion," but excluding any reference to the words "college," "alumni," and "cruise." Some search engines, such as Google and Fast Search, have word filters in their advanced search areas that allow you to force inclusion or exclusion of some words or phrases in your search. In other search engines, such as at Alta Vista, you need to structure a Boolean search using the operator words themselves and even to use parentheses for more complex searches, much as you did with mathematical equations in school.

In this case, you would enter the following in Alta Vista. (In this example, capital letters for the operators are used only to call attention to the operators themselves.):

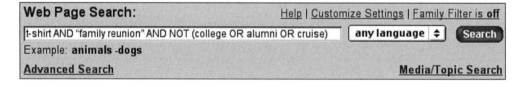

Most search engines will accommodate the use of some shortcut Boolean operators from their *simple search* area. For example, you could search for information about koala bears but you might want to exclude Teddy bears. Your simple search might be entered as follows:

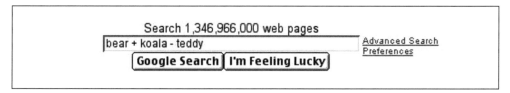

You could search specifically for koala bears and exclude Teddy bears another way by using a phrase:

The second search would narrow your search more than the first one by locating pages that include the words "koala" and "bear" adjacent to one another before excluding the pages with the word "teddy" in them.

The gist is that you often will start with a general search and then proceed to refine your search, perhaps several times, until you find the information you want in a quantity of search results you can reasonably review. You definitely want to read the Help text for the search engine(s) you use to properly understand how to make the most effective use of their facilities. In addition, the search engines also are enhanced from time to time. Whenever you visit one and see a new format or a new feature, review the Help or Search Tips text to see if anything has changed.

What about Using Directories?

Directories on the Internet are, as discussed earlier, compiled by human beings who decide what to include (or not include). Directories tend to be more limited in scope and content but may contain higher quality links. As mentioned, Yahoo! is the largest directory on the Web, although there are others. The Yahoo! site can be searched using either a simple or advanced search. When you search there, however, you may not locate as many matches as you would using one of the major search engines. This is because Yahoo! first searches its own directory database and presents Yahoo! matches. If there is no match, the search then reverts to an external search engine. (At the time of this writing, the external search engine Yahoo! used was Google, although other engines have been used in the past and still others may be used in the future.) In some cases, Yahoo! may present a combination of matches from its own database of directory entries *and* Web matches.

Some other directories of note are Lycos <http://www.lycos.com>, Excite http://www.excite.com>, and NBCi <http://www.nbci.com>. While the volume of content may not be as extensive as that found using search engines, you may certainly find additional resources through directories that might not ordinarily be indexed by the search engines. Such resources might include companies that sell party supplies, vendors that supply commemorative merchandise, companies that locate classmates and family members, mailing list services, and personal Web sites of families who have hosted or are planning to host their own family reunions.

The Ancestry.com Library

There are many specialized databases on the Internet. Few places, however, are as rich in reference content for genealogy and family history as Ancestry.com. In 2000, Ancestry.com indexed its vast collection of online columns and the archives of *Ancestry Magazine* and *Genealogical Computing*, and placed these materials in an online library. The library's contents are searchable and contain more than 300 articles concerning family reunions. Nowhere else on the Internet will you find more information and ideas about organizing and hosting family reunions, or gathering family history information at reunions.

The Ancestry.com library can be accessed from the top of its main Web page <http://www.ancestry.com> by clicking on the tab labeled Learn and then by clicking on the link to the Library. You can also go directly there by entering the Web address <http://www.ancestry.com/learn/library/main.htm>.

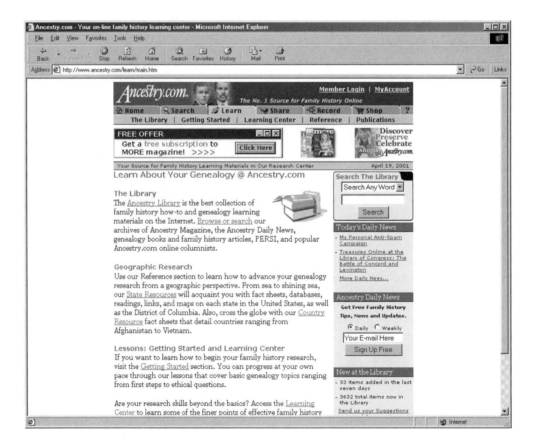

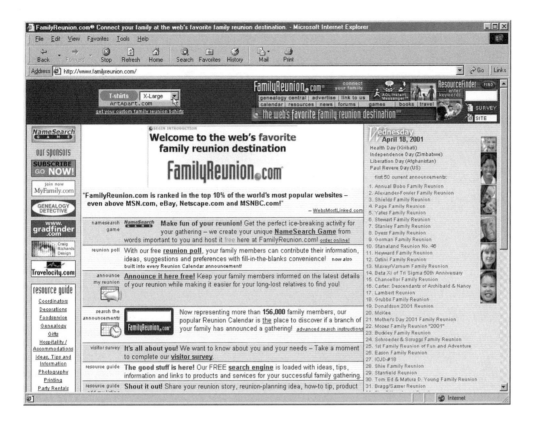

Publicizing Your Family Reunion on the Web

When you are organizing your reunion, you may want to publicize it to the outside world. There are some excellent ways to do so. RootsWeb has an online Family Reunion Calendar where you can post an announcement of your event. On its main page at <http://www.rootsweb.com>, look under the category of "Other Tools and Resources" for the link labeled "Calendars—Family Reunions/Events." It is simple to select the date, enter a text description of your event, and provide contact information.

FamilyReunion.com hosts a reunion announcement area at its Web site at <http://www.familyreunion.com/add>.

Some families post an announcement of their family reunion on one or more of the surname genealogy message boards on the Internet. MyFamily.com hosts message boards at <http://www.familyhistory.com>; RootsWeb hosts the GenConnect message boards at <http://genconnect.rootsweb.com/genbbs.cgi?search>; and Genealogy.com hosts the GenForum message boards at <http://genforum.genealogy.com>. All of these Web venues can be used to reach others who may be interested in more information concerning your family reunion.

You might also consider posting an announcement to the GEN-EVENTS-L mailing list. To do so, you must be a subscriber to the list. (You can learn how to subscribe at <http://lists.rootsweb.com/index/other/Miscellaneous/GEN-EVENTS.html>).

Building a Family Web Page at MyFamily.com

In Chapter 6, I discussed the MyFamily.com Web site. The Web site you create can be an excellent tool to publicize family reunions and, better still, promote ongoing family communication. At MyFamily.com you can build a free, custom family Web site for your family where you can share family history, photographs, recipes, data files, build and maintain a family address book, create a calendar of events (birthdays, anniversaries, and family reunions), and conduct real-time chats—by typing and/or with real voice communications. You or your family genealogist can even upload your family tree data from a genealogical software program and immediately create an Online Family Tree. The MyFamily.com site is located at <http://www.myfamily.com>. Simply select the link to build a Web site for your group or organization, enroll and begin creating the site. You can even share responsibility to build, update, and maintain information with family members if you authorize their access.

Summing Up

It is important that you invest the time to become familiar with the immense wealth of Internet resources. There are literally thousands of Web sites concerning family reunions where you can gather ideas about how to tailor your own family reunion. These include commercial sites with information about travel, hotels, commemorative products, planning services, caterers, photographers, DJs, transportation companies, and many other services discussed throughout the book. These and other Web sites will help you gather ideas about how to tailor our family reunion to *your* own group. By becoming an expert Web researcher, you can extend your imagination and become a more effective family reunion planner.

Family Reunion Worksheets

In This Appendix ✔

- Family Survey
- Family Contact Sheet
- Registration Form
- Reunion Planning Summary
- Reunion Announcement
- Registration Cover Letter
- Mailing Tracking Log
- Reunion Budget Spreadsheet
- Follow-up Letter
- Thank You Letter
- Reunion Evaluation
- Family Genealogy Correction

With any new project it is helpful to have a head start, and planning a family reunion is no different. Throughout this book I tried to present samples of forms, letters, spreadsheets, and other documents that illustrate the points I was describing. I believe that these can provide you with helpful templates for all types of communications, tracking, and calculations.

Your family reunion will be as unique as your collective family members are. Therefore, while all of the sample forms in this appendix will need some personalization to tailor them to your own family reunion, they can provide you with that necessary head start your need.

Feel free to use the sample forms in the following pages any way you like. Copy them and/or adapt them to you own needs. After all, why reinvent the wheel? Use them to create the best family reunion possible.

Family Reunion Survey

We are considering holding a family reunion for the descendants of John Paul Jones. In order to determine the interest level among the family and to begin developing a plan, we'd like to get your input concerning this event.

Please answer the questions below, and either mail it to Wally Jones at 123 Maple Lane, Family City, KS 55555 or send it to him via e-mail at wallyjones@address.com.

Your Name: _____

Your Address: _____

_____

Telephone: (____) _____-_____ E-mail: _____@_____

Number of persons in your family: _____

Are you interested in attending a family reunion?   YES   NO

What time of year is best for your family to attend? (Please indicate best month)
 JAN FEB MAR APR MAY JUNE JULY AUG SEPT OCT NOV DEC

Is there another time you would consider as a second choice? (Please indicate best alternative month)
 JAN FEB MAR APR MAY JUNE JULY AUG SEPT OCT NOV DEC

How many persons would be able to attend the reunion?
 Adults: _____   Children ages 0-6: _____   Children ages 7-12: _____
 Children ages 13-16: _____   Seniors: _____

We are considering having the reunion in Family City, Kansas, because there are so many family members located in that area. Would you attend the reunion if it were held there?   YES   NO

Are there any other areas you would consider as a site for the family reunion?
YES   NO   If so, where? _____

Would you and/or one of your family members be willing to participate on the planning committee for the reunion?   YES   NO   If so, who can participate?
_____

If you cannot help on the planning committee, would you and/or one of your family members be willing to help on-site at the reunion? YES   NO
If so, who can participate?

_____

Our reunion will include meals and some commemorative memento of the occasion. There will therefore be a per person cost to attend the reunion that we will communicate to you at a later date. There will be a price for adults and a lower price for children and seniors.

Thank you for your input to the process! We'll communicate the results back to you soon.

Wally Jones

Family Contact Sheet

Mr./Mrs./Miss/Ms./Dr./Other: _____

Last Name: _____ First Name: _____ MI: ____

Address #1: _____

Address #2: _____

Apt. # or Mail Drop : _____ Other Designation: _____

City: _____ State: _____ ZIP: _____-_____

Birth date: _____

Home Phone: (_____) _____-_____ Work Phone: (_____) _____-_____

Cellular Phone: (_____) _____-_____

E-mail Address: _____@_____

Web site: http://_____

Spouse's Name: _____ Birthdate: _____

E-mail Address: _____@_____

Children:

Name_____ Birthdate: _____

   E-mail Address: _____@_____

Name_____ Birthdate: _____

   E-mail Address: _____@_____

Name_____ Birthdate: _____

   E-mail Address: _____@_____

Name_____ Birthdate: _____

   E-mail Address: _____@_____

Registration Form

Name: _____

Address: _____

City: _____ State: _____ ZIP: _____

Telephone: (_____) _____ - _____ E-Mail: _____@_____

Full names of all family members who will be attending the family reunion and their ages. (Names should be listed as they should be printed on our name tags.)

Name: _____ Age: _____

Name: _____ Age: _____

Name: _____ Age: _____

Name: _____ Age: _____

Name: _____ Age: _____

Name: _____ Age: _____

Name: _____ Age: _____

Registration Fee - The per person registration fee for the reunion is $18.00. This amount will cover our estimated expenses.

Number of family members attending: _____ x $18.00 = $ _____ **(A)**

Meals - Our meal prices are based on the age of the person. Meals for children under 12 years of age and senior citizens over age 65 are $8.00; adults' meals are $12.00.

Number of children under age 12 _____ x $ 8.00 = $ _____

Number of adults _____ x $12.00 = $ _____

Number of senior citizens _____ x $ 8.00 = $ _____

TOTAL MEALS $ _____ **(B)**

T-Shirts: Commemorative T-shirts are available on a pre-event order basis. The deadline for the order is **February 28th**. They are made of 100% cotton and will be a pale teal color with our family reunion logo. The shirts come in sizes S, M, L, XL and XXL and are $7.50 each, sales tax included. Please indicate the number of shirts by size that you would like to purchase.

Small: _____ Medium: _____ Large: _____ X-Large: _____ XX-Large: _____

Total number of T-shirts: _____ x $ 7.50 = $ _____ (C)

If anyone in your family would like to take the optional trip to the amusement park, the admission price is $30.00 for adults and $18.00 for children under 12 years of age.   Please calculate the prices for your family and provide their names below.

Number of adults   _____ x $30.00 = $ _____

Number of children   _____ x $18.00 = $ _____

TOTAL = $ _____ (D)

Calculate your **total price** for the reunion by adding the dollar amounts labeled **(A)**, **(B)**, **(C)** and **(D)** and fill in the figure on the line below.

My total for the reunion is $ _____

Please return your registration in the enclosed self-addressed, stamped envelope, along with your check made out to *Wilson Family Reunion*, **no later than February 28th** to insure that your T-shirt order is placed. Contact Ricky Wilson by telephone at (312) 555-6666 or at rickywilson@abcmail.com with questions.

We'll look forward to seeing you in June!

Reunion Planning Summary

The following is a summary of the responses from our survey regarding our family reunion.

Preference for a place for the reunion:

Grandma Smith's house	8 responses
Aunt Elizabeth Weatherly's house	3 responses
Disney World in Orlando, FL	6 responses
Kansas City, MO (mid-point)	9 responses
No preference	1 response

Preference for time of year for the reunion:

June	11 responses
July	3 responses
August	9 responses
September	2 responses
No preference	2 responses

Estimated number of adults attending: 34

Estimated number of seniors attending: 13

Estimated number of children attending:

Ages 0-6		3
Ages 7-12		9
Ages 13-16		7
	Total =	19

People expressing a willingness in participating on the planning committee:

John Swords - Mailing list and invitations
Ed Smith - Accounting and finance
Laura Wilson - Catering and food., menus, etc.
John Alexander, Jr. - Willing to work with hotel
Cathy Wilson and Beth Smith - Decorations
Marie McKnitt - Family history and genealogy
Walt Weatherly, Sam Morgan, Emma Dale Holder, Edith Morgan, Peter Frank, Murray West, and Lydia Wilson - Willing to be assigned as needed

The following are some other ideas for the reunion:

Ideas regarding commemorative items:

T-shirt
Coffee mug
Sports water bottle
Group photograph

Suggested activities

Icebreaker games
Photo and heirloom display
Family history display
Pizza party for the younger set
Trip to see the old family home and the family cemetery
Softball, horseshoes, and badminton games
Banquet

Announcing

The MORGAN Family Reunion 2000

~~~~~~

**We're very happy to announce the third annual
MORGAN family reunion,
to be held this year at
fabulous DISNEY WORLD in Orlando, Florida!**

We surveyed the family and the results are in! The consensus is that we will meet at Walt Disney World for three days of family fun from July 28-30, 2000. We've negotiated an excellent, discounted rate with one of the Disney hotels and can obtain discounted multi-day admission tickets for everyone! While we're there, we'll also have a wonderful family banquet at the hotel.

Watch your mail for the registration packet which we'll be mailing within the next month. It will contain your registration form as well as details about the reunion, brochures about the attractions at Disney World, reservation instructions for the hotel, maps of the area, and information about local transportation. In addition, there will be ordering information for our annual commemorative reunion T-shirts.

**This year's reunion promises to be the best ever,
and you *don't* want to miss it!**

Mark your calendars NOW!

For questions, please contact Cousin Ed at (212) 555-5555.

Wilson Family Reunion

5619 S. Dorchester Avenue
Chicago, IL 60637

January 1, 2001

Greetings!

Happy New Year to you and your family! I hope you had a wonderful holiday season and that this letter finds everyone in good health.

You recently should have received your invitation to our Third Annual WILSON Family Reunion, scheduled for Saturday, June 23, 2001, at Promontory Point in Chicago. We're planning another exciting family get-together this year and want to make sure you're there to share the experience. It's not too early to begin making your plans now.

Enclosed is the registration form for your family and a self-addressed, stamped envelope. Please fill out the form and return it to me no later than **February 25th**. We will be ordering T-shirts to commemorate our reunion this year and ask that you get your registration form and payment in to us by that date so we can guarantee that everyone in your family gets one of these great shirts.

As in years past, we will have softball, soccer and frisbee competitions in the park for those so inclined and some special activities for the less athletically inclined in the pavilion. Our meal will be a family barbecue catered by Jimmy's Wonderful Barbecue. The meal prices are based on children, adult and senior citizen rates. In addition, you may bring a dessert to share with the family.

You don't want to miss our terrific family reunion. It has become a real tradition that everyone in the family looks forward to each year. If you have any questions, or if you would like to volunteer to help (and we always need volunteers to make the reunion a success!), please contact me by telephone at (312) 555-5555 or by e-mail at dwilson@email.net.

Mark your calendar and send in your registration form today! I can't wait to see you at the reunion!

Yours,

Della Wilson

Family Reunion Mailing Tracking Log

as of 10/1/2000

NAME	SURVEY	REC'D	ANNOUNCE	CONTACT	REC'D	F/U	REG. PKG.	REC'D	F/U	REMINDER
Alexander, John M.	5/10	5/22	6/19	5/10	5/22		6/20	7/1		9/2
DeJournette, Florence			6/19	6/20	7/15		6/20	7/15		9/2
Holder, Edward E.	5/10	5/30	6/19	5/10	5/30		6/20	7/3		9/2
Holder, Green Berry	5/18	6/3	6/19	5/18	6/3		6/20	6/27		9/2
Morgan, John Allen	5/10	5/21	6/19	5/10		7/1	6/20	8/18	8/1	9/2
Morgan, Samuel T.	5/10	5/29	6/19	5/10	5/29		6/20	8/7	8/1	9/2
Morgan, William R.	5/10		6/19	5/10	7/10	7/1	6/20	6/30		9/2
Smith, Andrew M.	5/10	6/1	6/19	5/10	6/1		6/20	6/30		9/2
Weatherly, Martin			6/19	7/1	7/15		6/20	7/11		9/2
Weatherly, Walton C.	5/10	5/22	6/19	5/10	5/22		6/20	7/22		9/2

Family Reunion Budget Spreadsheet

DESCRIPTION/VENDOR	UNIT DESCRIPTION	UNIT PRICE	EXTENSION
Telephone calls	Estimated 50 calls	$3.00	$150.00
Paper (reams)	6	7.50	45.00
Envelopes (cases)	8	11.00	88.00
Postage for mailings	45 families x 5 mailings	0.34	76.50
Hotel meeting room	Gardenia Room	250.00	250.00
Catering for banquet	Children & senior meals x 28	8.75	245.00
Catering for banquet	Adult meals x 72	11.00	792.00
T-shirts Galore!	Commemorative T-shirts	7.50	750.00
Supplies & equipment	Various	350.00	350.00
Accounting software	Quicken	85.00	85.00
Rockin' Robbie	Disk jockey	125.00	125.00
Pretty Flowers, Inc.	20 centerpieces for banquet	15.00	300.00
Julian's Party Supplies	Decorations	100.00	100.00
Photo Phil's Photography	Photography at banquet	75.00	75.00
			$3,431.50

Take $3,431.50 and subtract the meal figures of $245.00 and $792.00, leaving $2,394.50. This model assumes an attendance of 100 people, 28 of whom are childen or seniors. Divide $2394.50 by 100—a price of $23.95 per person—and add the per person meal price to this figure. Your per person prices, excluding any optional activities, are as follows:

Adults: **$34.95**
Children and seniors: **$32.70**

Registration Follow-Up Letter

May 1, 2000

Dear Cousin Richard,

    We're all very excited about our upcoming family reunion to be held at Disney World in Orlando, Florida, in July. I hope you received the announcement packet we mail to you almost two months ago. Since I have not yet heard from you or received registrations for your family, I wanted to write to ask if you have any questions about the reunion. You're all very important to us and we would love to have you join us for this great family event.

    I would be happy to send you another copy of the registration materials in the event you never received the packet or if it has been misplaced. Please let me know if you and your family will be able to make it to the reunion. You can reach me at (212) 555-5555 or by e-mail at cousined@abcdef.com. We would love to see an hope to hear from you soon!

Yours,

Cousin Ed

Family Reunion Evaluation

The reunion planning team worked hard to put together a fun and enjoyable event for the family. We know there are always things we could do to make the next reunion better and would like your feedback. Your name is optional.

Name: (optional) _____

How did you like the location where the reunion was held?

_____
_____

Should we consider the same place or something like it next year?   YES   NO

If NO, where would you suggest we hold our next reunion and what kind of facility should we consider?

_____
_____

On a scale of 1 to 5, with a 5 being the best, how would you rate the meals? _____

Was there something you really liked or disliked about the meals?

_____
_____

What was your favorite event at the reunion? _____

What was your *least* favorite event at the reunion? _____

On a scale of 1 to 5, with a 5 being the best, how would you rate the overall reunion?_____

What aspects of the reunion would you like us to keep next time? _____
_____

What improvements or changes would you like to see made for the next reunion?

_____
_____

Would you be willing to help plan and organize the next reunion?   YES   NO

If YES, please list your name and telephone number:
Name: _____ Telephone: (____) _____ - _____

THANK YOU FOR TAKING THE TIME TO GIVE US YOUR FEEDBACK

Thank You Letter

August 24, 2000

Dear Cousin Edith,

I just wanted to write to thank you for all of your help in making our family reunion a stunning success. It is always important for family to stick together and work together, and you really proved yourself a great member of our family team in everything you did. You did a wonderful job of organizing and managing the registrations and it all went very smoothly. We could not have put on as successful a reunion without your help.

Let's maintain the momentum we began while working together on the reunion and continue to keep in close touch. Please say hello to Tom and the kids for us.

Many thanks again.

Yours,

Cousin Ed

Family Genealogy Correction

Please provide any corrections to the family genealogy by completing the information below. As a conscientious family historian, I try to conduct scholarly and methodical research, and documentation of our family facts is important. Therefore, if you have original materials or copies of documentation that verifies the new/corrected information you are providing below, enclose photocopies for me. I will be happy to reimburse you for the costs of photocopying these materials. Thank you!

Name of individual: _____

What piece of information should be corrected? _____

Information as it appears in the record: _____

New/corrected information: _____

Where is the confirming documentation located? _____

_____

Do you have documentation that can be copied? (Bible records, birth, or death certificates, marriage licenses, wills, deeds, passports, naturalization papers, military records, Social Security information, etc.) _____

_____

_____

Your Name: _____ Tel. #: (____) _____-_____
Address: _____
City: _____ State: _____ ZIP: _____-_____
E-mail Address: _____@_____

You may mail this to me at:

John Doe
123 Maple Street
Anytown, NY 112233-1018

You can call me with any questions at: (555) 555-5555

My e-mail address is: johndoe@mailserver.net

Index

A

Access, 66
activities. *See* games/mixers
address books, family, 82–83, 90
Alta Vista, 77, 79
announcing your reunion, 84, 85, 91, 94–95
AnyWho, 74–75, 79
artifacts, displaying, 114
association directories, locating family members through, 73, 79
attendee packages, 100

B

budgets. *See* expenses, reunion

C

cameras, 118–19
catering expenses. *See* food
children's entertainers, working with, 43–44, 99
church halls, as reunion locations, 31
cleanup, organizing, 129
commemorative items
    confirming receipt of, 101
    distributing, 127
    expenses for, 47–48
    Internet resources for, 53
    tracking orders for, 64
communications
    announcing your reunion, 84, 85, 91, 94–95
    compiling a family address book, 82–83, 90
    defining a schedule for, 90–92
    developing a plan for, 81–82
    getting feedback after your reunion, 129–30, 131, 133–35
    hype mailings, 87–88, 92
    Internet resources for, 94–95
    looking toward the next reunion, 136–37
    obtaining contact information, 84
    producing a registration package, 84–87, 91, 95
    sample scenario for, 90–92
    setting up a family Web page, 137
    setting up a reunion Web page, 88–90
    soliciting input, 1–4, 83–84, 90
    during your reunion, 124–26
communications expenses
    Internet resources for, 53
    mailing costs, 29–30, 53
    photocopying costs, 29, 53
    telephone charges, 29
    using e-mail, 30
contact information
    family address books, 82–83, 90
    information needed, 56–58
    systems for recording, 58–59
costs, figuring. *See* expenses, reunion
cruises
    Internet resources for, 11
    as reunion locations, 8, 33–34

D

dates, selecting
    advantages of summertime, 8
    considering weather, 8–9
    importance of, 8
decorations, 44–46, 101
details, managing. *See* logistical details, managing
directories, locating family members through, 73, 79
disc jockeys, working with, 42–43

E

e-mail, 30, 82
Emailing List Pro, 68
entertainers, working with, 43–44, 99
evaluating your reunion

importance of, 129–30
Internet resources for, 131
planning your next reunion, 135–37
summarizing results, 133, 135
using questionnaires, 129–30, 133–35
See also input, soliciting
Excel, 66
Excite PeopleFinder, 75, 79
expenses, reunion
    assigning expense category responsibilities, 28
    assigning information-gathering duties, 27–28
    catering/food expenses, 35–37, 53
    choosing a treasurer, 28
    commemorative items, 47–48, 53
    communications expenses, 29–30, 53
    decorations, 44–46
    developing budgets
        balancing expenditures and income, 50–51
        involving team members, 49–50
        preparing a spreadsheet, 48–49
    hired personnel expenses, 39–44, 53
    importance of good planning, 27
    Internet resources for, 53
    location expenses, 30–34, 53
    office supplies/equipment, 48
    permit/license expenses, 34–35
    preparing a final accounting report, 133
    and reunion size/scope, 28
    setting registration fees, 50, 51
    signage, 46–47
    transportation expenses, 37–39
    See also record-keeping

F

family address books, 82–83, 90
family contact information. *See* contact information
family events, organizing reunions around, 8
family history
    displaying family artifacts, 114
    displaying family photographs, 114–15
    enlisting the help of family historians, 113
    gathering genealogical data at reunions
        collecting information, 116–18
        making preparations for, 116
        recommended tools, 118–19
    Internet resources for, 121
    sharing family stories, 120
Family Information Scavenger Hunt, 104–5
family newsletters, 136–37
Family Origins Version 8.0 Deluxe, 66

Family Reunion Organizer, 66
family stories, sharing, 120
FastSearch, 77, 79
feedback, getting. *See* evaluating your reunion;
    input, soliciting
financial records
    preparing reports, 52, 133
    setting up a filing system, 52, 62
    software for, 48, 51, 62
    tools needed for, 51–52
    See also expenses, reunion
Find Yourself activity, 108
first-aid kits, 101
florists, 53, 99
flyers, 124–26
food
    avoiding duplication of courses, 63
    combining home-cooked and catered foods, 36
    controlling costs, 35–36
    importance of food and meal information, 62
    managing food events, 127–28
    organizing banquets, 63, 128
    reviewing food plans, 98–99
    working with caterers, 36–37, 53
FoxPro, 67

G

games/mixers
    Family Information Scavenger Hunt, 104–5
    Find Yourself activity, 108
    "I'm My Own Grandpa" activity, 106–7
    Internet resources for, 110
    outdoor games, 108–9
    recognition awards, 105–6
    Secret Word activity, 107–8
    tennis ball game, 106
    "Three New Friends" game, 105
    Who's That? activity, 107
genealogy. *See* family history
Google™, 77, 79

H

holiday trip sites, as reunion locations, 7–8
hometowns, as reunion locations, 6
hospitality events, 127
hosts, appointing, 101
HotBot, 77, 79
hotels
    Internet resources for, 53
    as reunion locations, 31–33, 97–98

I

icebreakers. *See* games/mixers
"I'm My Own Grandpa" activity, 106–7
infoUSA.com, 76, 79
input, soliciting
    to determine the mix of the group, 3
    evaluating responses, 3–4
    importance of, 1
    in person/by phone, 3
    recording responses, 3–4
    using questionnaires, 2–4, 83–84, 90
    See also evaluating your reunion
Internet resources
    association directories, 73, 79
    caterers, 53
    commemorative items, 53
    cruise reunions, 11
    evaluating your reunion, 131
    florists, 53
    games/mixers, 110
    hotels as reunion locations, 53
    invitations, 94–95
    mailing costs, 53
    maps, 11
    organizing your reunion, 24
    parks as reunion locations, 11
    photocopying costs, 53
    photographers, 53
    ranches as reunion locations, 11
    recreational facilities as reunion locations, 11
    registration forms, 95
    resorts as reunion locations, 10
    reunion locations, 10–11
    search engines, 77, 79
    sharing family history, 121
    ski trip reunions, 11
    telephone search facilities, 74–77, 79
    travel and travel agents, 10
    videographers, 53
Internet search engines, 77, 79
investigators, locating family members using, 77–78

L

LabelPro 3.0, 69
license/permit expenses, 34–35
locating family members
    combining several approaches, 78
    hiring a professional investigator, 77–78
    minimum information needed for, 71
    through other family members, 72
    using association directories, 73
    using Internet search engines, 77, 79

    using Internet search tools, 74–77, 79
locations for reunions
    big cities as, 7
    church halls as, 31
    cruise reunions, 8, 11, 33–34
    holiday trip sites as, 7–8
    hotels as, 31–33, 53, 97–98
    importance of, 6
    Internet resources for, 10–11, 53
    parks as, 7, 11, 30–31, 34–35, 98
    ranches as, 8, 11
    recreational facilities as, 7, 11, 30–31, 34–35, 98
    resorts as, 7, 10, 33
    reunions in conjunction with special family events, 8
    selecting an in-between location, 6–7
    ski trip reunions, 8, 11
    using the family hometown, 6
    vacation sites as, 7–8
    and weather conditions, 8–9
logistical details, managing
    distributing commemorative items, 127
    hosting hospitality events, 127
    keeping people informed, 124–26
    locating people at your reunion, 123
    managing food events, 127–28
    managing transportation, 128–29
    organizing cleanup, 129
    setting up a registration desk, 126–27
    signage, 46–47, 101, 124
    using sign-up sheets, 123–24
Lotus 1-2-3, 66

M

mailings
    computerized lists for, 82–83
    costs for, 29–30, 53
    importance of tracking, 59
    keeping a log, 60
Mail Them, 69
management, reunion. *See* logistical details, managing
maps, Internet resources for, 11
meals. *See* food
memorabilia. *See* commemorative items
mixers. *See* games/mixers
MyFamily.com, 89–90, 137

N

nametags, 100, 103–4
newsletters, 124–26, 136–37

O

office supplies/equipment, 48
organizing your reunion
    building your team
        identifying team members, 16
        making contact, 16–17
        setting a meeting date/time, 17
    doing it alone *vs.* involving family members, 13–14
    establishing a committee structure, 20–21
    expanding your team, 20–21
    Internet resources for, 24
    meeting for the first time
        assigning responsibilities, 20
        encouraging participation, 18
        identifying task assignments, 18–20
        preparing an agenda, 17–18
        reviewing input, 17
        setting goals, 17
    planning the next reunion, 135–37
    receiving status reports, 22
    setting a timeline, 21–22
    summarizing input, 14–15
outdoor games, 108–9

P

parks
    Internet resources for, 11
    as reunion locations, 7, 30–31, 34–35, 98
PeopleFinder, 75, 79
People Pages, 74, 79
People Search, 76, 79
permit/license expenses, 34–35
Personal Mailing List, 68
personnel expenses
    children's entertainers, 43–44
    disc jockeys, 42–43
    Internet resources for, 53
    photographers, 39–41, 53
    videographers, 41–42, 53
photocopying costs, 29, 53
photographers
    Internet resources for, 53
    working with, 39–41, 99
photographs, displaying, 114–15
planning your reunion. *See* organizing your reunion
professional investigators, locating family members using, 77–78

Q

questionnaires
    for post-reunion feedback, 129–30, 131, 133–35
    for pre-reunion input, 2–4, 83–84
Quicken®, 62, 67

R

ranches
    Internet resources for, 11
    as reunion locations, 8
recognition
    after your reunion, 135
    awards, 105–6
    keeping records for, 65
record-keeping
    commemorative item orders, 64
    family contact information, 56–59
    financial records, 48, 51–52, 62
    food and meal information, 62–63
    importance of, 55
    Internet resources for, 68–69
    keeping it simple, 55
    mailing records, 59–60
    registration records, 60–61
    software for, 66–69
    special events and transportation, 64–65
    for special recognition, 65
recreational facilities
    Internet resources for, 11
    as reunion locations, 7, 30–31, 34–35, 98
registration desks, 100, 126–27
registration fees, 50, 51
registration packages
    contents of, 86–87
    importance of, 84–86
    Internet resources for, 95
    mailing, 85
    tracking responses to, 87, 91
registration records
    disseminating information from, 61
    information on, 60–61
    systems for, 61
resorts
    Internet resources for, 10
    as reunion locations, 7, 33
reunion logistics. *See* logistical details, managing
Reunion Planner, 69

S

Scavenger Hunt, Family Information, 104–5
search engines, Internet, 77, 79
Secret Word activity, 107–8

Send It, 68
signage, 46–47, 101, 124
sign-up sheets, using, 123–24
site preparation/set-up
    appointing hosts, 101
    assembling attendee packages, 100
    confirming receipt of commemorative
        items, 101
    contacting park rangers, 98
    creating a checklist for, 97
    making nametags, 100, 103–4
    meeting with entertainers, 99
    meeting with hotel staff, 97–98
    meeting with transportation carriers,
        99–100
    placing decorations, 101
    preparing a first-aid kit, 101
    putting up signage, 101
    reconfirming with florists, 99
    reconfirming with photographers and
        videographers, 99
    reviewing food plans, 98–99
    setting up a welcome area, 100
size of your reunion
    determining the best size, 4–6
    large reunions, 5–6
    medium-sized reunions, 5
    small reunions, 5
ski trip reunions, 8, 11
special events, keeping records of, 64–65
steno pads, 118
SuperPages.com's People Pages, 74, 79
surveys. *See* questionnaires
Switchboard, 75, 79

T

tape recorders, 118
telephone charges, 29
tennis ball game, 106
"Three New Friends" game, 105
timing. *See* dates, selecting
transportation
    managing, 128–29
    meeting with carriers, 99–100
transportation expenses
    record-keeping systems for, 64–65
    reimbursing committee member
        expenses, 37–38
    during the reunion, 38–39
travel and travel agents, Internet resources for,
    10–11

U

Ultimates, The, 76–77, 79

V

vacation sites, as reunion locations, 7–8
video cameras, 119
videographers
    Internet resources for, 53
    working with, 41–42, 99

W

Web pages
    family, 137
    reunion
        advantages of, 88–89
        finding free space for, 88
        using the MyFamily.com site, 89–90
welcome areas, 100, 126–27
Who's That? activity, 107
WhoWhere, 76, 79

Y

Yahoo! People Search, 76, 79

About the Author

George G. Morgan has been working on his own family genealogy since he was a ten-year-old in North Carolina. His aunt and grandmother sparked his interest by recounting stories about their early years, about family traditions, and about prominent colonial ancestors. He became engrossed by the contents of dozens of boxes of letters, family papers, Bibles, deeds and photographs in his grandmother's home, and soon became the family historian and archivist.

Mr. Morgan, a former large-event planner for a subsidiary of IBM, is president of Aha! Seminars, Inc., a Florida-based company that works almost exclusively with library cooperatives and consortia in providing continuing education to library employees and professionals. The company teaches people to use Microsoft's *Windows* and the Netscape Internet browser, Web page design, collection development, and a variety of high-tech topics. In addition, Mr. Morgan teaches "Genealogy for Librarians: How to Best Serve Your Genealogy Patrons" and a variety of genealogy workshops for library personnel, genealogical societies, groups, and individuals. He conducted his first annual genealogy cruise for more than one hundred genealogists in February 2001 and is already planning another cruise for 2002.

His highly popular genealogy column, "Along Those Lines …", appears on the Ancestry.com Web site and in the *Ancestry Daily News*, which has a current weekly circulation of over one million subscribers. He also writes the "Genealogy Tip of the Day" which appears on the Emazing.com Web site and is available via e-mail.

Mr. Morgan has published a number of cover articles in the quarterly *Genealogical Computing* where his articles have won him critical praise. He is a regular contributor to *Ancestry* Magazine and *Southern Queries* magazine, and has been published in many other genealogical publications in the United States and Canada. His first book, *The Genealogy Forum on America Online: The Official User's Guide*, was published in 1998 (Ancestry, SLC). He is working on a new book about how to organize and conduct effective cemetery research.

He is a frequent speaker at genealogical societies' meetings and conferences, and has been invited to help work on preparations for the Federation of Genealogical Societies' annual conference to be held in Florida in 2003.